CROCHET
ANIMAL RUGS

Over 20 crochet patterns for fun
floor mats and matching accessories

Ira Rott

CONTENTS

INTRODUCTION

Get creative and transform your child's room into a
magical modern bedroom inspired by animals!

Crochet rugs are the perfect place for your children to
read and play. They make a great conversation piece
with a unique style. This collection of animal rugs
includes adorable matching pillows and other coordinating
accessories that will bring any home to life.

You can decorate your craft room or nursery with items
from this book and spend only a few evenings making
each piece. So no need to wait, just get your hooks
and yarn ready to begin a fun crochet adventure!

HOW TO USE THIS BOOK

SKILL LEVELS

Each pattern in this book has been assigned a skill level, ranging from beginner to challenging. To get comfortable with a project, pick a pattern that suits your skill level, and then move up to the next level as you learn new stitches and techniques.

Beginner – Best choice for novice crocheters. These patterns are written using basic stitches and techniques, with minimal shaping and simple assembly.

Moderate – These patterns include basic and moderate stitches, such as treble crochet (tr), popcorn stitch (PC), reverse single crochet (rsc) and picot. There are simple color changes and shaping with repetitive stitch patterns. Easy assembly might involve hand-sewing and blocking.

Challenging – Be ready for some challenging step-by-step assembly and more complex pattern repeats. These patterns may include basic lace, irregular curves, unique shapes and techniques. Increased level of concentration might be required for some parts of these patterns.

SIZE AND GAUGE

Every pattern specifies the finished size based on the gauge, yarn weight and hook size. The gauge is the number of stitches and rows per 4in x 4in (10cm x 10cm) square. This number might be crucial for some patterns and forgiving for others.

Checking the gauge is always beneficial for the final measurements. For instance, if you are using the suggested yarn weight and hook size but crochet too tight, then the number of stitches and rows per 4in x 4in (10cm x 10cm) square will be greater and your finished item will be smaller. The opposite effect will occur if you crochet too loose. To calibrate the gauge, use a larger or smaller size hook.

If the size is not important, you can use any yarn with any suitable size hook and your finished measurements will vary depending on the gauge. For example, you can make a doily or a wall decoration from a rug pattern by using thin yarn instead of thick yarn (see General Techniques: Wall Decoration).

TIPS

- If you are new to crochet, start with a beginner level pattern. For example, make a beginner level pillow base (see Common Shapes) and then choose a moderate level pillow pattern to finish the remaining parts.

- Try a moderate level rug pattern before attempting to make a challenging rug.

- Ensure that you are familiar with stitches and techniques listed for each pattern before starting (see Useful Information, Crochet Techniques and General Techniques).

- If you are a left-handed crocheter, please refer to the tips in the Crochet Techniques section (see Crochet Techniques: Left-Handed Crochet).

READING PATTERNS

Crochet patterns in this book are written using American (US) terminology. This means that if you follow UK terminology then you need to convert the terms to British (UK) terminology (see Useful Information: Crochet Terminology).

- "Work in rows" means – crochet a row of stitches as indicated in the pattern, then turn your work to begin the next row. The pattern will specify which rows are on right side (RS) and wrong side (WS).

- "Work in the round" means – begin with a magic ring/foundation ring or work along both sides of the foundation chain (see Crochet Techniques). Crochet each round as indicated in the pattern without turning, then join the last stitch to the first stitch. Always work with right side (RS) facing, unless otherwise indicated.

- "Work in spiral rounds" means – begin with a magic ring/foundation ring or work across both sides of the foundation chain (see Crochet Techniques). Crochet the first round as indicated in the pattern without turning and without joining. Work the beginning stitch of each round into first stitch of the previous round; never join rounds. Work spiral rounds with right side (RS) facing, unless otherwise indicated.

- The total stitch count is indicated after the equal sign (=) at the end of each row/round. The beginning chain(s) might be counted as stitch(es) or not, as marked at the beginning of the rows/rounds. Some instructions apply to multiple rows/rounds, for example Ch 1 (does not count as a st now and throughout).

READING CHARTS

A crochet chart is an illustration featuring special symbols to represent stitches. Charts help to visualize patterns before you start crocheting. The beginning of the work is marked with a small black arrow. Different colors indicate each row/round along with the row/round number. If the chart has more than 2 colors, a color key will be provided. To understand a chart, refer to the symbol key (see Useful Information: Abbreviations).

The use of charts is optional. You can choose to follow a chart or the pattern text, or even use both.

The charts shown in this book are for right-handed crochet and show your work on the right side (RS). If the chart begins on the left, it means the first row is on the wrong side (WS).

TOOLS AND MATERIALS

CROCHET HOOKS

Various sizes of crochet hooks are required for these projects. We have listed the metric and US sizes with the project instructions, but you can use this conversion chart for reference to quickly find the correct size for your region.

Metric	US letter	US number	Canada/UK
3.75mm	F	5	9
4.25mm/4.5mm	G	6/7	8/7
5mm	H	8	6
5.5mm	I	9	5
6mm	J	10	4
6.5mm	K	10.5	3
9mm	M/N	13	00

YARN

All of these projects are made using medium weight yarn (weight 4). However, you will notice instructions for using 1, 2 or 3 strands throughout the book. See Crochet Techniques for tips on how to work with several strands of yarn at once.

If you struggle working with multiple strands, simply substitute 2 strands of medium yarn (weight 4) with 1 strand of bulky yarn (weight 5), or 3 strands of medium yarn (weight 4) with 1 strand of super bulky yarn (weight 6).

US	UK	Australia	Meters per 100g
Medium (4)	Aran	10-ply	150-199
Bulky (5)	Chunky	12-ply	100-149
Super Bulky (6)	Super Chunky	14-ply	60-99

The amount of yarn is given in yards/meters for each color of medium weight yarn (weight 4). "Small amount" means less than 93yd (85m) of yarn.

Please keep in mind that the finished size and the total yarn length may vary depending on the materials used and the gauge.

Yarn weight is the thickness of yarn, which may vary from country to country. Use the conversion chart provided to find the correct yarn for your region.

OTHER EQUIPMENT

You will also need the following equipment to create the projects in this book:

- Stitch markers – for marking stitches and indicating the start of the round
- Spray bottle – useful for wet blocking
- Tapestry needle(s) or latch hook – for sewing and weaving in ends
- Scissors
- Blocking board or interlocking play mat – for wet blocking
- Polyester stuffing or bed pillow filler
- Clips – for holding pieces in place while sewing

RUG LINING

I recommend adding a non-slip lining to crochet rugs to ensure that they stay in place. To do this, you will require the following additional equipment:

- Basic straight stitch sewing machine
- Non-adhesive shelf liner with grip or rug gripper pad
- Hook and loop tape (strip with hooks only) – 1in (2.5cm) wide
- All-purpose sewing thread

WALL HANGING

To transform your crocheted designs into wall art, you will require the following equipment:

- Size 10 crochet thread – approximately 875yd (800m)
- 1.9mm (US size 5) steel hook
- Wall frame or poster frame at least 3in (7.6cm) larger than the finished wall decoration on each side
- Matboard backing that fits in frame
- Matboard edging that fits in frame
- Chenille needle with sharp point
- Finger guard (thimble)
- Fabric stiffener or corn starch
- Rust-proof straight pins
- Scotch tape or packing tape

JEFFERY THE ELEPHANT

Rug, Pillow and Stool Cover

Jeffery is my most favorite animal creation! His amazing curved trunk reminds me of hooks and inspires me to crochet. It is not surprising that I chose to make this elephant collection to decorate my craft studio – the combination of texture, lace and chunkiness brings my workspace to life!

After making Jeffery in gray yarn, I just had to make a colorful friend for him! So I crocheted Josefina in a pretty pink yarn with a purple bow. Choose your favorite (or make both) and, once you've completed the rug, crochet a coordinating elephant pillow and a sweet stool cover to decorate your room.

ELEPHANT RUG

SKILL LEVEL

FINISHED SIZE
52in x 31½in (132cm x 80cm)

HOOKS
5.5mm (I), 6.5mm (K), 9mm (M/N)

YARN WEIGHT
4

NUMBER OF STRANDS
1, 2 and 3

**GAUGE WITH 3 STRANDS
AND 9MM (M/N) HOOK**
9 dc x 4.5 rows = 4in x 4in (10cm x 10cm)

STITCH SUMMARY
Ch, sl st, sc, sc2tog, hdc, dc, dc2tog, tr,
picot, PC, beg PC, crest, shell, arch, join

SKILLS
Working in rows and in the round,
raw edge finishing, working across
the bottom of the foundation chain,
blocking, sewing

LEFT-HANDED CROCHET
See Crochet Techniques:
Left-Handed Crochet

YARN

Abbreviation	Color	Amount
MC	Gray or Pink	2187-2515yd (2000-2300m)
CC1	Black	Small amount
CC2	White	Small amount
CC3	Lilac or Pink (optional)	93-109yd (85-100m)

HEAD AND TRUNK

Make 1. Begin by working in the round with a 9mm (M/N) hook and 3 strands of **MC**.

STEP 1 - HEAD

To beg: Ch 3, sl st in third ch from hook to form a ring (or start with a magic ring)

Rnd 1: Ch 2 (does not count as a st from now to Rnd 11), 12 dc in ring; join = 12 sts

Rnd 2: Ch 2, 2 dc in same st as join, 2 dc in next 11 sts; join = 24 sts

Rnd 3: Ch 2, dc in same st as join, 2 dc in next st, [dc in next st, 2 dc in next st] 11 times; join = 36 sts

Rnd 4: Ch 2, 2 dc in same st as join, dc in next 2 sts, [2 dc in next st, dc in next 2 sts] 11 times; join = 48 sts

Rnd 5: Ch 2, dc in same st as join, dc in next 2 sts, 2 dc in next st, [dc in next 3 sts, 2 dc in next st] 11 times; join = 60 sts

Rnd 6: Ch 2, 2 dc in same st as join, dc in next 4 sts, [2 dc in next st, dc in next 4 sts] 11 times; join = 72 sts

Rnd 7: Ch 2, dc in same st as join, dc in next 4 sts, 2 dc in next st, [dc in next 5 sts, 2 dc in next st] 11 times; join = 84 sts

Rnd 8: Ch 2, 2 dc in same st as join, dc in next 6 sts, [2 dc in next st, dc in next 6 sts] 11 times; join = 96 sts

Rnd 9: Ch 2, dc in same st as join, dc in next 6 sts, 2 dc in next st, [dc in next 7 sts, 2 dc in next st] 11 times; join = 108 sts

Rnd 10: Ch 2, 2 dc in same st as join, dc in next 8 sts, [2 dc in next st, dc in next 8 sts] 11 times; join = 120 sts

Rnd 11: Ch 2, dc in same st as join, dc in next 8 sts, 2 dc in next st, [dc in next 9 sts, 2 dc in next st] 11 times; join = 132 sts

Do not break off yarn. Continue to work **Step 2** in rows.

HEAD AND TRUNK CHART

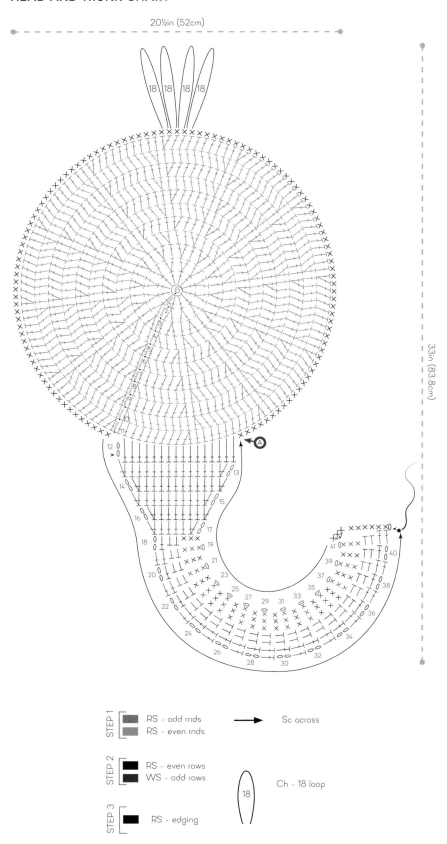

20½in (52cm)

33in (83.8cm)

STEP 1		
	RS - odd rnds	
	RS - even rnds	

→ Sc across

STEP 2		
	RS - even rows	
	WS - odd rows	

Ch - 18 loop

STEP 3		
	RS - edging	

STEP 2 - TRUNK

Row 12: (RS) Ch 2 (counts as first dc now and throughout), skip st with join, dc in next 16 sts, place **Marker A** in next st; turn = 17 sts

Row 13: (WS) Ch 2, skip first st, dc2tog, dc in next 12 sts, dc2tog; turn = 15 sts

Row 14: (RS) Ch 2, skip first st, dc2tog, dc in next 10 sts, dc2tog; turn = 13 sts

Row 15: (WS) Ch 2, skip first st, dc2tog, dc in next 8 sts, dc2tog; turn = 11 sts

Row 16: (RS) Ch 2, skip first st, dc2tog, dc in next 6 sts, dc2tog; turn = 9 sts

Row 17: (WS) Ch 2, skip first st, dc2tog, dc in next 4 sts, dc2tog; turn = 7 sts

Row 18: (RS) Ch 2, skip first st, dc in next st, hdc in next 2 sts, sc in next 3 sts; turn = 7 sts

Row 19: (WS) Ch 1 (does not count as a st), sc in first st, sc in next 2 sts, hdc in next 2 sts, dc in next 2 sts; turn = 7 sts

Rows 20-41: Repeat Rows 18 and 19 in established pattern, ending on WS

Turn and work **Step 3** on RS.

STEP 3 - EDGING

With RS facing, ch 1 (does not count as a st), sc in first st, sc in next 5 sts, 3 sc in next st, sc evenly across the concave edge of the trunk, sc in st with **Marker A** and remove the marker, sc in next 55 sts, [ch 18, sc in next st] 4 times, sc in next 55 sts, sc evenly across the convex edge of the trunk; join (1)

Fasten off, leaving a long single strand of **MC** for sewing. Weave in the other ends.

LEFT EAR CHART

31½in (80cm)

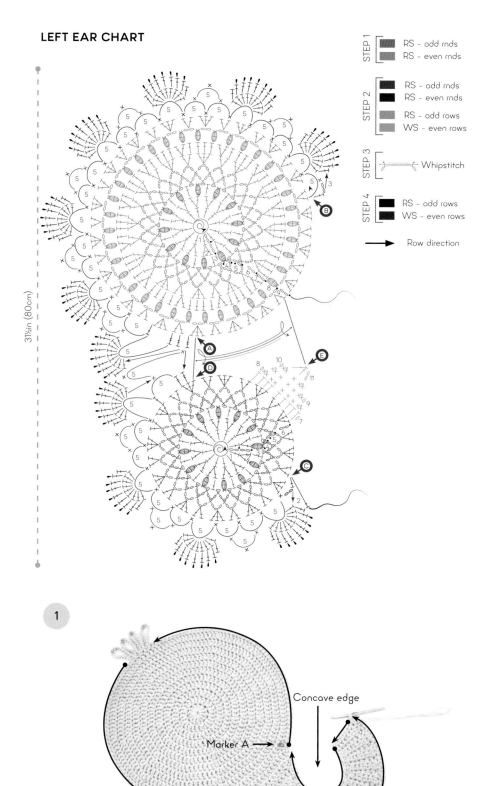

STEP 1		RS - odd rnds
		RS - even rnds
STEP 2		RS - odd rnds
		RS - even rnds
		RS - odd rows
		WS - even rows
STEP 3		Whipstitch
STEP 4		RS - odd rows
		WS - even rows

→ Row direction

Concave edge

Marker A →

Convex edge

LEFT EAR

Make 1. Work with a 9mm (M/N) hook and 3 strands of **MC**.

STEP 1 - BIG CIRCLE

Work in the round to make 1 big circle.

To beg: Ch 3, sl st in third ch from hook to form a ring (or start with a magic ring)

Rnd 1: Ch 2 (does not count as a st now and throughout), 12 dc in ring; join = 12 sts

Rnd 2: Ch 2, 2 dc in same st as join, 2 dc in next 11 sts; join = 24 sts

Rnd 3: Beg PC in same st as join, ch 1, dc in next st, ch 1, [PC in next st, ch 1, dc in next st, ch 1] 11 times; join = 12 PC and 12 dc

Rnd 4: Ch 1 (does not count as a st now and throughout), [skip PC, sc in next ch-1 sp, ch 3, skip dc, sc in next ch-1 sp, ch 3] 12 times; join = 24 arches

Rnd 5: Sl st in first ch of the first arch, ch 1, sc in same arch, [ch 3, sc in next arch] 23 times, ch 3; join = 24 arches

Rnd 6: Ch 2, [3 dc in next arch, 2 dc in next arch] 12 times; join = 60 sts

Rnd 7: Ch 2, dc in same st as join, dc in next 3 sts, 2 dc in next st, [dc in next 4 sts, 2 dc in next st] 11 times; join = 72 sts

Rnd 8: Beg PC in same st as join, ch 2, skip st, [PC in next st, ch 2, skip st] 35 times; join = 36 PC

Rnd 9: Ch 2, [skip PC, 3 dc in next ch-2 sp, skip PC, 2 dc in next ch-2 sp] 18 times, place **Marker A** in 14th st to the right, place **Marker B** in 14th st to the left; join = 90 sts

Fasten off, leaving a long single strand of **MC** for sewing. Weave in the other ends.

STEP 2 - SMALL CIRCLE

Make 1 small circle by following the instructions for the big circle from the beginning to Rnd 6 (see Left Ear: Step 1 - Big Circle). Place **Marker C** in 7th st to the right and continue to work the tip in rows as follows:

Row 7: (RS) Ch 1 (does not count as a st now and throughout), hdc in same st as join, hdc in next 8 sts, place **Marker D** in 7th st to the left; turn = 9 sts

Row 8: (WS) Ch 1, do not skip first st, sc2tog, sc in next 5 sts, sc2tog; turn = 7 sts

Row 9: (RS) Ch 1, do not skip first st, sc2tog, sc in next 3 sts, sc2tog; turn = 5 sts

Row 10: (WS) Ch 1, do not skip first st, sc2tog, sc in next st, sc2tog; turn = 3 sts

Row 11: (RS) Ch 2 (counts as first dc), skip first st, dc2tog, place **Marker E** in st just made = 2 sts

Fasten off and weave in the ends.

STEP 3 - ASSEMBLING CIRCLES

With RS of both circles facing you, place the small circle right up against the big circle with **Marker D** below **Marker A** and **Marker E** below the long tail of the big circle (2). Using the long tail from the big circle, whipstitch towards **Marker A** to join the small circle from **Marker E** to **Marker D** (3). Turn to WS and whipstitch across the same edges. Weave in the end. Do not remove markers.

STEP 4 - EDGING

With RS of the ear facing you, join yarn in st with **Marker B** of the big circle.

Row 1: (RS) Working from **Marker B** towards **Marker A**, [ch 5, skip 2 sts, sc in next st] 18 times, ch 5, skip 2 sts, dc in next st, ch 5, skip 2 sts, tr in next 3 sts, skip **Marker A** and **Marker D**, tr in next 2 sts of small circle, ch 5, skip 2 sts, dc in next st, [ch 5, skip 2 sts, sc in next st] 10 times, ch 2, skip 2 sts, dc in st with **Marker C** (counts as last arch); turn = 32 arches (4)

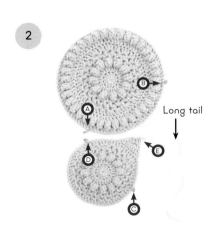

Long tail

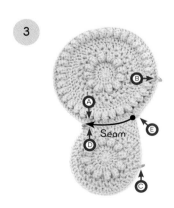

Seam

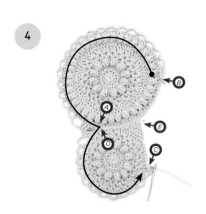

Row 2: (WS) Skip ch-2 sp, [9 dc in next arch, sc in next arch, ch 5, sc in next arch] 3 times, 9 dc in next arch, sc in next arch, ch 5, skip 2 tr, sc in next tr, skip 2 tr, [9 dc in next arch, sc in next arch, ch 5, sc in next arch] 6 times, 9 dc in next arch, sc in next arch, ch 2, dc in st with **Marker B** (counts as last arch); turn = 11 shells and 11 arches

Row 3: (RS) Skip ch-2 sp, [crest across next shell, sc in next arch] 10 times, crest across next shell, dc in st with **Marker C** = 11 crests

Fasten off, leaving a long single strand of **MC** for sewing. Weave in the other ends. Remove all markers. Spray block the shell edge or wet block the entire ear if necessary (see General Techniques: Blocking).

RIGHT EAR

Make 1. Work with a 9mm (M/N) hook and 3 strands of **MC**.

STEP 1 - BIG CIRCLE

Follow the instructions for the big circle from the Left Ear (see Left Ear: Step 1 - Big Circle).

STEP 2 - SMALL CIRCLE

Follow the instructions for the small circle from the Left Ear (see Left Ear: Step 2 - Small Circle).

STEP 3 - ASSEMBLING CIRCLES

With RS of both circles facing you, place the small circle right up against the big circle with **Marker C** below **Marker B**, and **Marker E** below the long tail of the big circle (5). Using the long tail from the big circle, whipstitch towards **Marker B** to join the small circle from **Marker E** to **Marker C** (6). Turn to WS and whipstitch across the same edges. Weave in the ends. Do not remove markers.

STEP 4 - EDGING

With RS of the ear facing you, join yarn in st with **Marker D** of the small circle.

Row 1: (RS) Working from **Marker D** towards **Marker C**, [ch 5, skip 2 sts, sc in next st] 10 times, ch 5, skip 2 sts, dc in next st, ch 5, skip 2 sts, tr in next 2 sts, skip **Marker C** and **Marker B**, tr in next 3 sts of big circle, ch 5, skip 2 sts, dc in next st, [ch 5, skip 2 sts, sc in next st] 18 times, ch 2, skip 2 sts, dc in st with **Marker A** (counts as last arch); turn = 32 arches (7)

Row 2: (WS) Skip ch-2 sp, [9 dc in next arch, sc in next arch, ch 5, sc in next arch] 6 times, 9 dc in next arch, skip 2 tr, sc in next tr, ch 5, skip 2 tr, sc in next arch, [9 dc in next arch, sc in next arch, ch 5, sc in next arch] 3 times, 9 dc in next arch, sc in next arch, ch 2, dc in st with **Marker D** (counts as last arch); turn = 11 shells and 11 arches

Row 3: (RS) Skip ch-2 sp, [crest across next shell, sc in next arch] 10 times, crest across next shell, dc in st with **Marker A** = 11 crests

Fasten off, leaving a long single strand of **MC** for sewing. Weave in the other ends. Remove all markers. Spray block the shell edge or wet block the entire ear if necessary (see General Techniques: Blocking).

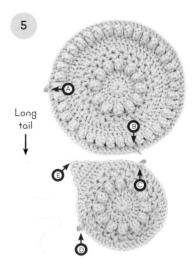

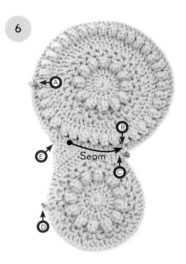

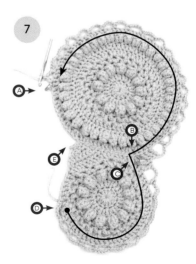

EYES

Make 2. Follow the instructions for the basic eyes (see Common Shapes: Basic Eyes). Use 2 strands of **CC1** with a 9mm (M/N) hook for the pupils and 1 strand of **CC2** with a 5.5mm (I) hook for the highlights.

TUSKS (OPTIONAL)

Make 2. Work in rows with a 6.5mm (K) hook and 2 strands of **CC2**.

To beg: Ch 11

Row 1: (WS) Sl st in second ch from hook (the skipped ch does not count as a st), sc in next 2 chs, hdc in next 3 chs, dc in next 4 chs; turn = 10 sts

Row 2: (RS) Ch 1 (does not count as a st), sc in next 10 sts, 2 sc in end ch, continuing working across the bottom of the foundation ch, sc in next 10 sts = 22 sts

Fasten off, leaving a long single strand of **CC2** for sewing. Weave in the other ends.

BOW (OPTIONAL)

Make 1. Follow the instructions for the big bow (see Common Shapes: Big Bow). Use 3 strands of **CC3** with a 9mm (M/N) hook.

RIGHT EAR CHART

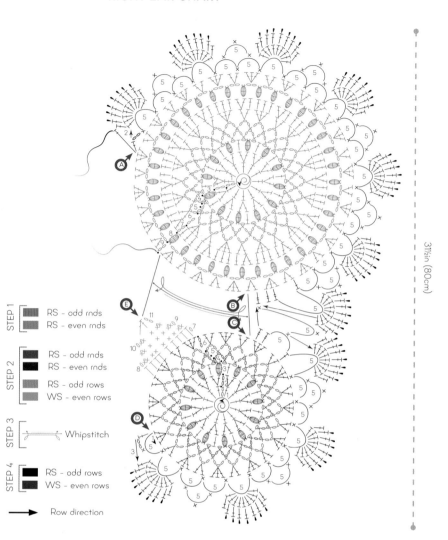

STEP 1		RS – odd rnds
		RS – even rnds
STEP 2		RS – odd rnds
		RS – even rnds
		RS – odd rows
		WS – even rows
STEP 3		Whipstitch
STEP 4		RS – odd rows
		WS – even rows

→ Row direction

3½in (80cm)

TUSK CHART

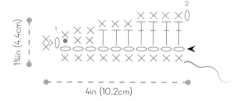

1¾in (4.4cm)

4in (10.2cm)

ASSEMBLING RUG

Place the eyes approximately 3 rounds above the edge on each side of the head (8).

To position the eyebrows (optional), cut 2 x 5in (12.7cm) lengths of any color yarn and place them above the eyes to reflect a facial expression. Place a marker on each end of both yarn guides (8).

Backstitch the eyes around the edge using the long **CC1** tail from the eyes. Thread the needle with a double strand of **CC1** and chain stitch the eyebrows between the markers (9), removing markers as you go.

If using, place the tusks on each side of the trunk and whipstitch across RS and WS using the long **CC2** tail from the tusks (10).

With RS facing, place the ears right up against the head, 8-9 stitches apart from the top loops on each side. Using the long **MC** tail from the ears, whipstitch across the inner edge of the ears on RS (11) and WS (12).

The tip of the curved trunk should overlap onto the ear, but do not worry if it doesn't as everyone crochets differently. Leave the trunk unattached or whipstitch the corner of the trunk to the ear on RS and WS using the long MC tail from the trunk (11 and 12).

For Josefina, place the bow onto the head and backstitch around the center with 1 strand of **CC3** (13). Leave the side edges of the bow unattached or whipstitch the corners to keep them in place.

If desired, make a removable non-slip lining (see General Techniques: Non-Slip Lining).

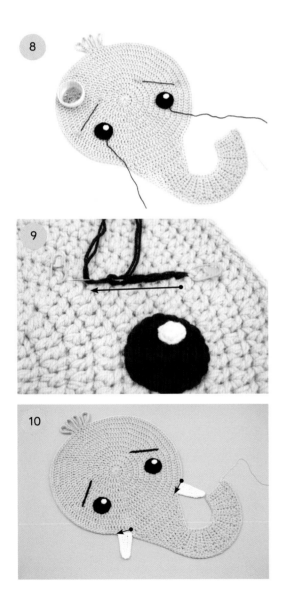

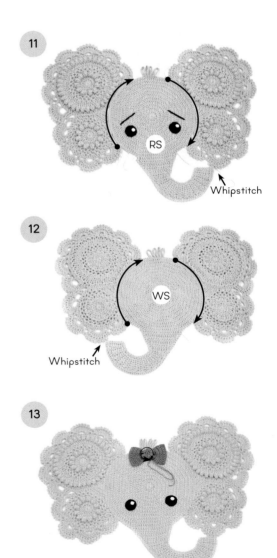

Use light pink yarn to create Josefina.

ELEPHANT PILLOW

SKILL LEVEL

FINISHED SIZE
26in x 17½in (66cm x 44.5cm)

HOOKS
3.75mm (F), 4.25mm (G), 5.5mm (I)

YARN WEIGHT
4

NUMBER OF STRANDS
1

**GAUGE WITH 1 STRAND
AND 5.5MM (I) HOOK**
14 sc x 16 rows = 4in x 4in (10cm x 10cm)

STITCH SUMMARY
Ch, sl st, sc, sc3tog, bpsc, hdc, dc,
dc2tog, dc3tog, picot, PC, beg PC, join

SKILLS
Working in rows and in the round,
raw edge finishing, sewing

LEFT-HANDED CROCHET
Fully compatible

YARN

Abbreviation	Color	Amount
MC	Light Gray	842-930yd (770-850m)

Contrasting colors are the same as for the
Elephant Rug (small amount of each).

HEAD PILLOW BASE

Make 1 front and 1 back using 1 strand of **MC** with a 5.5mm (I) hook. Follow the instructions for the round pillow base (see Common Shapes: Round Pillow Base). Fasten off after finishing the back piece, but do not break off yarn after finishing the front piece.

Holding the front and the back pieces together with WS facing each other, work the joining round through both pieces of fabric at the same time using the working yarn from the front piece.

Rnd 26: Ch 1 (does not count as a st), sc in same st as previous sl st, sc in next 75 sts, [ch 18, sc in next st] 5 times, sc in next 60 sts, stuff the pillow (1), sc in next 15 sts; join = 156 sts and 5 loops

Fasten off and weave in the ends.

EYES

Make 2. Follow the instructions for the basic eyes (see Common Shapes: Basic Eyes). Work with a 4.25mm (G) hook using 1 strand of **CC1** for the pupils and 1 strand of **CC2** for the highlights.

BOW (OPTIONAL)

Make 1. Follow the instructions for the small bow (see Common Shapes: Small Bow). Use 1 strand of **CC3** with a 3.75mm (F) hook.

EARS

Make 2 front and 2 back pieces following the same instructions. Work in rows with a 5.5mm (I) hook and 1 strand of **MC**.

STEP 1 - FRONT AND BACK

To beg: Ch 39

Row 1: (RS) Sc in second ch from hook (the skipped ch does not count as a st), place **Marker A** in skipped ch, sc in next 11 sts, [2 sc in next st, sc in next 12 sts] 2 times; turn = 40 sts

Row 2: (WS) Ch 3 (counts as first dc now and throughout), dc in first st, dc in next 19 sts, 2 dc in next st, dc in next 18 sts, 2 dc in next st; turn = 43 sts

Row 3: (RS) Ch 3, skip first st, dc in next st, [ch 2, skip st, PC in next st] 19 times, ch 2, skip st, dc in next 2 sts; turn = 19 PC and 4 dc

Row 4: (WS) Ch 3, skip first st, dc in next st, 2 dc in next ch-2 sp, skip PC, 2 dc in next ch-2 sp, [skip PC, 3 dc in next ch-2 sp, skip PC, 2 dc in next ch-2 sp] 9 times, dc in next 2 sts; turn = 53 sts

Row 5: (RS) Ch 3, skip first st, dc in next st, [ch 2, skip st, PC in next st] 24 times, ch 2, skip st, dc in next 2 sts; turn = 24 PC and 4 dc

Row 6: (WS) Ch 3, skip first st, dc in next st, *3 dc in next ch-2 sp, skip PC, [2 dc in next ch-2 sp, skip PC] 2 times**, repeat 7 more times from * to **, 3 dc in next ch-2 sp, dc in next 2 sts; turn = 63 sts

Row 7: (RS) Ch 3, skip first st, dc in next st, [ch 2, skip st, PC in next st] 29 times, ch 2, skip st, dc in next 2 sts; turn = 29 PC and 4 dc

Row 8: (WS) Ch 3, skip first st, dc in next st, [2 dc in next ch-2 sp, skip PC] 29 times, 2 dc in next ch-2 sp, dc in next 2 sts; turn = 64 sts

Row 9: (RS) Ch 3, skip first st, dc2tog, PC in next st, [ch 2, skip st, PC in next st] 12 times, dc in next st, dc3tog, place **Marker B** in next st; turn = 13 PC and 4 dc

Row 10: (WS) Ch 3, skip first st, dc in next st, [skip PC, 2 dc in next ch-2 sp] 12 times, skip PC, dc2tog; turn = 27 sts

Row 11: (RS) Ch 3, skip first st, dc2tog, skip st, PC in next st, [ch 2, skip st, PC in next st] 9 times, skip st, dc in next st, dc2tog; turn = 10 PC and 4 dc

Row 12: (WS) Ch 3, skip first st, dc in next st, [skip PC, 2 dc in next ch-2 sp] 9 times, skip PC, dc2tog = 21 sts

Fasten off and weave in the ends.

STEP 2 - FRONT AND BACK

With RS facing, join **MC** in stitch with **Marker B** and work the next row across the remaining stitches of Row 8 as follows:

Row 9: (RS) Ch 3, skip st with **Marker B**, dc3tog, PC in next st, [ch 2, skip st, PC in next st] 12 times, dc in next st, dc2tog; turn = 13 PC and 4 dc

Rows 10-12: Repeat Rows 10-12 of the front and back (see Ears: Step 1 - Front and Back).

Fasten off and weave in the ends.

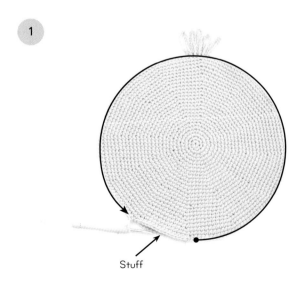

1

Stuff

STEP 3 - ASSEMBLING EARS

Place the front and the back pieces of each ear together with WS facing each other. Use clips to hold the layers of fabric in place for joining (2). Do not use straight basting pins as they can easily get lost in the pillow.

To join the layers, work around the outer edge of the ear with 1 strand of **MC** and a 5.5mm (I) hook, inserting the hook through both pieces of fabric at the same time. Join yarn in stitch with **Marker A** of front piece, ch 1 to beg, [2 sc, picot] repeat evenly around the edge working towards **Marker B** of both pieces, then towards **Marker A** of back piece (3). Do not join the inner edge of the ear.

Fasten off, leaving a long tail for sewing. Remove all markers.

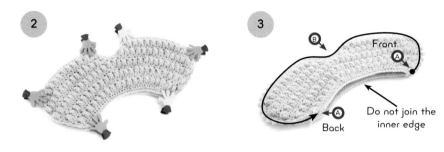

EAR CHART

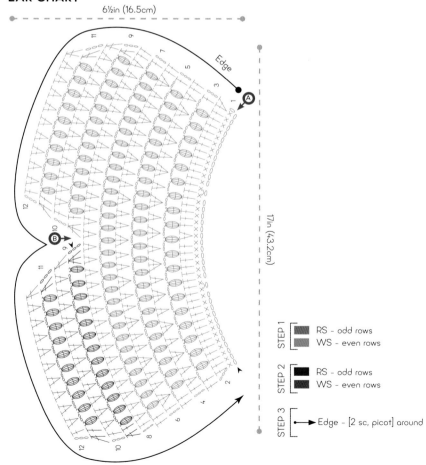

6½in (16.5cm)

17in (43.2cm)

STEP 1	RS - odd rows
	WS - even rows
STEP 2	RS - odd rows
	WS - even rows
STEP 3	Edge - [2 sc, picot] around

TRUNK

Make 1. Work in the round with a 4.25mm (G) hook and 1 strand of **MC**. Stuff the trunk as you go, using a moderate amount of polyester stuffing (do not over-stuff, as stuffing may show through the stitches).

To beg: Ch 3, sl st in third ch from hook to form a ring (or start with a magic ring)

Rnd 1: Ch 1, (does not count as a st now and throughout), 6 sc in ring; join = 6 sts

Rnd 2: Ch 1, 2 sc in same st as join, 2 sc in next 5 sts; join = 12 sts

Rnd 3: Ch 1, 2 sc in same st as join, 2 sc in next 11 sts; join = 24 sts

Rnd 4: Ch 1, bpsc in same st as join, bpsc in next 23 sts; join = 24 sts

Rnds 5-24: Ch 1, sc in same st as join, sc in next 3 sts, hdc in next 4 sts, dc in next 8 sts, hdc in next 4 sts, sc in next 4 sts; join = 24 sts

Rnd 25: Ch 1, hdc in same st as join, 2 hdc in next st, [hdc in next st, 2 hdc in next st] 11 times; join = 36 sts

Rnd 26: Ch 1, sc in same st as join, sc in next 5 sts, hdc in next 6 sts, dc in next 12 sts, hdc in next 6 sts, sc in next 6 sts; join = 36 sts

Rnd 27: Ch 1, hdc in same st as join, hdc in next st, 2 hdc in next st, [hdc in next 2 sts, 2 hdc in next st] 11 times; join = 48 sts

Rnd 28: Ch 1, hdc in same st as join, hdc in next 47 sts; join = 48 sts

Fasten off, leaving a long tail for sewing.

ASSEMBLING PILLOW

Place the ears right up against the head on each side, approximately 10 stitches apart from the top loops. Using the long **MC** tail from the ears, whipstitch around entire edge, sandwiching the pillow edge in between the layers of the ears (4 and 5).

Place the trunk 4-5 rounds below the center of the head and whipstitch around the edge using the long **MC** tail from the trunk (6).

Whipstitch the tip of the trunk to the head using **MC** to keep it in place (7).

Place the eyes on each side above the trunk and backstitch around the edge using the long **CC1** tail from the eyes (8).

To position the eyebrows (optional), cut 2 x 3in (7.6cm) lengths of any color yarn and place them above the eyes to reflect a facial expression. Place a marker on each end of both yarn guides. Thread the needle with **CC1** and chain stitch the eyebrows between the markers (8), removing markers as you go. Jeffery is now completed.

For Josefina, place the bow onto the head and backstitch around the center using the long **CC3** tail from the bow (9).

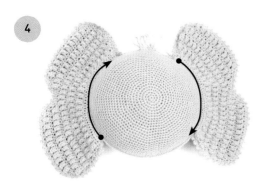

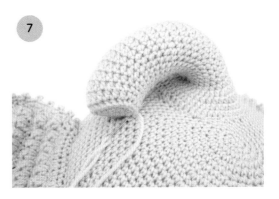

ELEPHANT STOOL COVER

SKILL LEVEL

FINISHED SIZE
12in-13½in (30.5cm-34.3cm) diameter

HOOK
9mm (M/N)

YARN WEIGHT
4

NUMBER OF STRANDS
3

GAUGE WITH 3 STRANDS AND 9MM (M/N) HOOK
9 dc x 4.5 rows = 4in x 4in (10cm x 10cm)

STITCH SUMMARY
Ch, sl st, sc, dc, PC, beg PC, arch, join

SKILLS
Working in the round

LEFT-HANDED CROCHET
Fully compatible

YARN

Abbreviation	Color	Amount
MC	Light Gray	361-394yd (330-360m)

STOOL COVER

Make 1. Work in the round with a 9mm (M/N) hook and 3 strands of **MC**. Follow the instructions for the big circle of the Elephant Rug from the beginning to Rnd 6 (see Left Ear: Step 1 - Big Circle). Work the remaining rounds as follows:

Rnd 7: Beg PC in same st as join, ch 2, skip st, [PC in next st, ch 2, skip st] 29 times; join = 30 PC

Rnd 8: Ch 1, skip beg PC, sc in next ch-2 sp, ch 3, [sc in next ch-2 sp, ch 3] 29 times; join = 30 arches

Rnds 9-11: Sl st in first ch of the first arch, ch 1, sc in same arch, [ch 3, sc in next arch] 29 times, ch 3; join = 30 arches

Fasten off and weave in the ends.

DRAWSTRING

Make 1. Work with a 9mm (M/N) hook and 3 strands of **MC**.

To beg: Ch 4

Row 1: (RS) *2 dc in fourth ch from hook (3 skipped chs count as first dc), ch 3 (counts as dc), sl st in same ch as previous dc**, ch 179, repeat once from * to ** = 175 chs with 4 dc on each end

Fasten off and weave in the ends.

ASSEMBLING STOOL COVER

Using a crochet hook, thread the drawstring through the arches of the final round of stool cover (1) and tie when ready to use.

Repeat
Rnds 9-11 if
alterations
are needed.

RUSTY THE GIRAFFE

Rug, Pillow and Security Blanket

Africa's tallest freckled mammals roam the Savannah; they are truly gentle giants. Giraffes are enchanting creatures, so interesting to watch and admire. You do not have to travel to Africa when you can have a safari in your own room.

This precious collection of a rug, a pillow and a security blanket will make any nursery room fun and adorable! A complex appearance of colorwork in the giraffe skin print is created by simply changing the colors for alternate rows. You will be amazed by how effortless this beautiful texture is.

GIRAFFE RUG

SKILL LEVEL

FINISHED SIZE
38in x 40in (96.5cm x 101.6cm)

HOOK
9mm (M/N)

YARN WEIGHT
4

NUMBER OF STRANDS
2 and 3

**GAUGE WITH 3 STRANDS
AND 9MM (M/N) HOOK**
9 dc x 4.5 rows = 4in x 4in (10cm x 10cm)

STITCH SUMMARY
Ch, sl st, sc, rsc, hdc, dc, dc3tog,
tr, PC, beg PC, FDC, OS, shell,
OS over shell, arch, join

SKILLS
Working in rows and in the round,
raw edge finishing, working across
the bottom of the foundation chain,
changing colors, blocking, sewing

LEFT-HANDED CROCHET
See Crochet Techniques:
Left-Handed Crochet

YARN

Abbreviation	Color	Amount
MC	Yellow	710-820yd (650-750m)
CC1	Warm Brown	710-820yd (650-750m)
CC2	Oatmeal	710-820yd (650-750m)
CC3	Black	Small amount
CC4	White	Small amount
CC5	Any color for bow (optional)	93-109yd (85-100m)

EARS

Make 2. Work in rows with a 9mm (M/N) hook and 3 strands of **MC**.

To beg: Ch 7

Row 1: (WS) OS in fourth ch from hook (3 skipped chs count as dc), skip ch, OS in next ch, place **Marker A** in last ch, dc in same ch with marker; turn = 2 OS and 2 dc

Row 2: (RS) Ch 3 (counts as first dc now and throughout), OS over shell, (dc, ch 1, dc) in sp between shells, OS over shell, dc in last st; turn = 2 OS and 4 dc

Row 3: (WS) Ch 3, OS over shell, ch 2, skip dc, OS in next ch-1 sp, ch 2, skip dc, OS over shell, dc in last st; turn = 3 OS and 2 dc

Row 4: (RS) Ch 3, OS over shell, ch 2, 9 dc in center of next shell, ch 2, OS over shell, dc in last st; turn = 2 OS, 1 shell and 2 dc

Row 5: (WS) Ch 3, OS over shell, ch 1, work across the next shell [dc in next st, ch 1] 9 times, OS over shell, dc in last st; turn = 2 OS and 11 dc

Row 6: (RS) Ch 3, OS over shell, [ch 3, skip dc, sc in next ch-1 sp] 8 times, ch 3, skip dc, OS over shell, dc in last st; turn = 2 OS, 9 arches and 2 dc

Row 7: (WS) Ch 3, OS over shell, ch 3, skip arch, [sc in next arch, ch 3] 7 times, skip arch, OS over shell, dc in last st; turn = 2 OS, 8 arches and 2 dc

Row 8: (RS) Ch 3, OS over shell, ch 3, skip arch, [sc in next arch, ch 3] 6 times, skip arch, OS over shell, dc in last st; turn = 2 OS, 7 arches and 2 dc

Row 9: (WS) Ch 3, OS over shell, ch 3, skip arch, [sc in next arch, ch 3] 5 times, skip arch, OS over shell, dc in last st; turn = 2 OS, 6 arches and 2 dc

Row 10: (RS) Ch 3, OS over shell, ch 3, skip arch, [sc in next arch, ch 3] 4 times, skip arch, OS over shell, dc in last st; turn = 2 OS, 5 arches and 2 dc

Row 11: (WS) Ch 3, OS over shell, ch 3, skip arch, [sc in next arch, ch 3] 3 times, skip arch, OS over shell, dc in last st; turn = 2 OS, 4 arches and 2 dc

Row 12: (RS) Ch 3, OS over shell, ch 3, skip arch, [sc in next arch, ch 3] 2 times, skip arch, OS over shell, dc in last st; turn = 2 OS, 3 arches and 2 dc

Row 13: (WS) Ch 3, OS over shell, ch 3, skip arch, sc in next arch, ch 3, skip arch, OS over shell, dc in last st; turn = 2 OS, 2 arches and 2 dc

Row 14: (RS) Ch 3, OS over shell, skip 2 arches, OS over shell, dc in last st; turn = 2 OS and 2 dc

Row 15: (WS) Ch 3, 2 dc in center of next OS, ch 1, 2 dc in center of next OS, dc in last st; turn = 6 sts

Row 16: (RS) Skip 3 dc, OS in next ch-1 sp, skip 2 dc, sl st in last st = 1 OS and 1 sl st

Fasten off and weave in the ends.

Edge: Use the same yarn and hook as for the ears. Join yarn in st with **Marker A** and remove the marker. Ch 1 (does not count as a st), sc evenly across the edge towards the top corner, 3 sc in top corner, sc evenly across the remaining edge. Do not work across the bottom edge.

Fasten off, leaving a long single strand of **MC** for sewing. Weave in the other ends. Spray block the ears (see General Techniques: Blocking).

EAR CHART

15½in (39.4cm)

RS – even rows
WS – odd rows
Sc across

HEAD

Make 1. Work in rows with a 9mm (M/N) hook and 3 strands of yarn, changing colors (**MC** and **CC1**) as indicated in the pattern.

NOTE: Ch-2 sps are not included in the total stitch count.

To beg: With **CC1**, ch 59

Row 1: (WS) Sc in second ch from hook (the skipped ch does not count as a st), hdc in next ch, dc in next 2 chs, tr in next 2 chs, dc in next 2 chs, hdc in next ch, sc in next ch, [ch 2, skip 2 chs, sc in next ch, hdc in next ch, dc in next 2 chs, tr in next 2 chs, dc in next 2 chs, hdc in next ch, sc in next ch] 4 times; change to **MC** and turn = 50 sts

Row 2: (RS) With **MC**, Ch 1 (does not count as a st now and throughout), sc in first st, sc in next 9 sts, [dc in next 2 chs of the foundation row below, sc in next 10 sts] 4 times; turn = 58 sts

Row 3: (WS) Ch 1, sc in first st, sc in next 57 sts; change to **CC1** and turn = 58 sts

Row 4: (RS) With **CC1**, ch 3 (counts as first dc now and throughout), skip first st, dc in next st, hdc in next st, sc in next st, [ch 2, skip 2 sts, sc in next st, hdc in next st, dc in next 2 sts, tr in next 2 sts, dc in next 2 sts, hdc in next st, sc in next st] 4 times, ch 2, skip 2 sts, sc in next st, hdc in next st, dc in next 2 sts; turn = 48 sts

Row 5: (WS) Ch 3, skip first st, dc in next st, hdc in next st, sc in next st, [ch 2, skip ch-2 sp, sc in next st, hdc in next st, dc in next 2 sts, tr in next 2 sts, dc in next 2 sts, hdc in next st, sc in next st] 4 times, ch 2, skip ch-2 sp, sc in next st, hdc in next st, dc in next 2 sts; change to **MC** and turn = 48 sts

Row 6: (RS) With **MC**, ch 1, sc in first st, sc in next 3 sts, *[FDC in next sc two rows below] 2 times, skip ch-2 sp, sc in next 10 sts**, repeat 3 more times from * to **, [FDC in next sc two rows below] 2 times, skip ch-2 sp, sc in next 4 sts; turn = 58 sts

Row 7: (WS) Ch 1, sc in first st, sc in next 57 sts; change to **CC1** and turn = 58 sts

Row 8: (RS) With **CC1**, ch 1, sc in first st, hdc in next st, dc in next 2 sts, tr in next 2 sts, dc in next 2 sts, hdc in next st, sc in next st, [ch 2, skip 2 sts, sc in next st, hdc in next st, dc in next 2 sts, tr in next 2 sts, dc in next 2 sts, hdc in next st, sc in next st] 4 times; turn = 50 sts

Row 9: (WS) Ch 1, sc in first st, hdc in next st, dc in next 2 sts, tr in next 2 sts, dc in next 2 sts, hdc in next st, sc in next st, [ch 2, skip ch-2 sp, sc in next st, hdc in next st, dc in next 2 sts, tr in next 2 sts, dc in next 2 sts, hdc in next st, sc in next st] 4 times; change to **MC** and turn = 50 sts

Row 10: (RS) With **MC**, ch 1, sc in first st, sc in next 9 sts, *[FDC in next sc two rows below] 2 times, skip ch-2 sp, sc in next 10 sts**, repeat 3 more times from * to **; turn = 58 sts

Row 11: (WS) Ch 1, sc in first st, sc in next 57 sts; change to **CC1** and turn = 58 sts

Rows 12-19: Repeat Rows 4-11

Rows 20-25: Repeat Rows 4-9

Row 26: (RS) Repeat Row 10, carrying **CC1** across 6 sts at the beg of the row

Row 27: (WS) Sl st in first st, sl st in next 5 sts, ch 1, sc in next 46 sts; change to **CC1** and turn = 52 sts

Row 28: (RS) With **CC1**, ch 1, sc in first st, hdc in next st, dc in next 2 sts, tr in next 2 sts, dc in next 2 sts, hdc in next st, sc in next st, [ch 2, skip 2 sts, sc in next st, hdc in next st, dc in next 2 sts, tr in next 2 sts, dc in next 2 sts, hdc in next st, sc in next st] 3 times; turn = 40 sts

Row 29: (WS) Ch 1, sc in first st, hdc in next st, dc in next 2 sts, tr in next 2 sts, dc in next 2 sts, hdc in next st, sc in next st, [ch 2, skip ch-2 sp, sc in next st, hdc in next st, dc in next 2 sts, tr in next 2 sts, dc in next 2 sts, hdc in next st, sc in next st] 3 times; change to **MC** and turn = 40 sts

Row 30: (RS) With **MC**, ch 1, carrying **CC1** across 6 sts at the beg of the row, sc in first st, sc in next 9 sts, *[FDC in next sc two rows below] 2 times, skip ch-2 sp, sc in next 10 sts**, repeat 2 more times from * to **; turn = 46 sts

Row 31: (WS) Sl st in first st, sl st in next 5 sts, ch 1, sc in next 34 sts; change to **CC1** and turn = 40 sts

Row 32: (RS) With **CC1**, ch 1, sc in first st, hdc in next st, dc in next 2 sts, tr in next 2 sts, dc in next 2 sts, hdc in next st, sc in next st, [ch 2, skip 2 sts, sc in next st, hdc in next st, dc in next 2 sts, tr in next 2 sts, dc in next 2 sts, hdc in next st, sc in next st] 2 times; turn = 30 sts

Row 33: (WS) Ch 1, sc in first st, hdc in next st, dc in next 2 sts, tr in next 2 sts, dc in next 2 sts, hdc in next st, sc in next st, [ch 2, skip ch-2 sp, sc in next st, hdc in next st, dc in next 2 sts, tr in next 2 sts, dc in next 2 sts, hdc in next st, sc in next st] 2 times; change to **MC**, break off **CC1** and turn = 30 sts

Row 34: (RS) With **MC**, ch 1, sc in first st, sc in next 9 sts, *[FDC in next sc two rows below] 2 times, skip ch-2 sp, sc in next 10 sts**, repeat one more time from * to ** = 34 sts

Fasten off and weave in the ends.

ASSEMBLING HEAD

STEP 1 - SC EDGING

Work with a 9mm (M/N) hook and 3 strands of **MC**. With RS facing, begin working from the bottom right corner: Beg sc evenly around the edge towards the bottom left corner, placing 3 sc in each top corner for increasing. Do not work across the bottom edge.

Enlarge the last loop temporarily to secure the work from unraveling, but do not fasten off. Spray block the head (see General Techniques: Blocking).

STEP 2 - SEWING EARS

Place the ears right up against the top corners of the head. Whipstitch around the edge on RS and WS using the long **MC** tail from the ears (1).

STEP 3 - RSC EDGING

With RS facing, insert the hook through the large loop at the bottom left corner and reduce the size of the loop to normal. Working with a 9mm (M/N) hook and using the attached yarn, ch 1, rsc around the head and the ears towards the bottom right corner (2). Fasten off and weave in the ends.

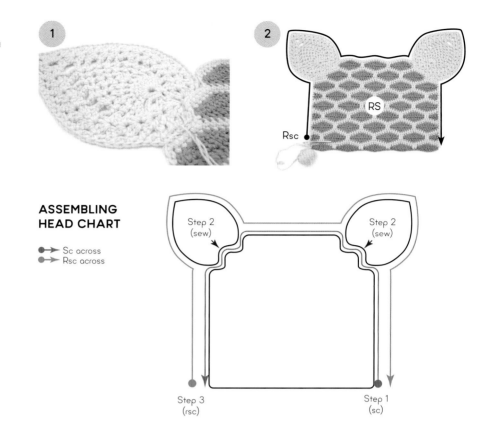

ASSEMBLING HEAD CHART

➤●➤ Sc across
●➤ Rsc across

Step 2 (sew)

Step 2 (sew)

Step 3 (rsc)

Step 1 (sc)

HEAD CHART

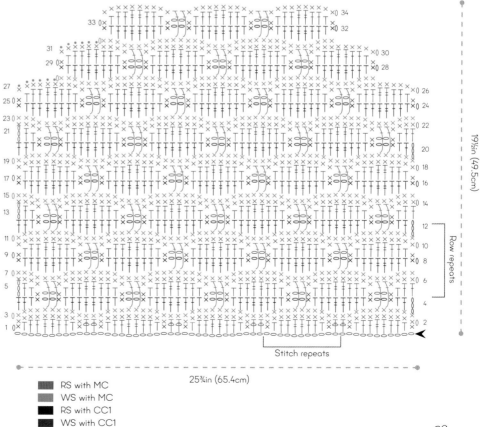

19½in (49.5cm)

Row repeats

Stitch repeats

25¾in (65.4cm)

▮ RS with MC
▮ WS with MC
■ RS with CC1
▮ WS with CC1

29

MUZZLE

Make 1. Work in the round with a 9mm (M/N) hook and 3 strands of **CC2**.

To beg: Ch 53

Rnd 1: Dc in third ch from hook (2 skipped chs do not count as a st), dc in next 49 chs, 6 dc in last ch, continue working across the bottom of the foundation ch, dc in next 49 chs, 5 dc in last ch; join = 110 sts

Rnd 2: Ch 2 (does not count as a st now and throughout), 2 dc in same st as join, dc in next 24 sts, 3 dc in next st (**bottom point**), dc in next 24 sts, 2 dc in next 6 sts, dc in next 23 sts, dc3tog (**center top**), dc in next 23 sts, 2 dc in next 5 sts; join = 122 sts

Rnd 3: Ch 2, 2 dc in same st as join, dc in next 26 sts, 3 dc in next st (**bottom point**), dc in next 26 sts, 2 dc in next st, [dc in next st, 2 dc in next st] 5 times, dc in next 22 sts, dc3tog (**center top**), dc in next 22 sts, [2 dc in next st, dc in next st] 5 times; join = 134 sts

Rnd 4: Ch 2, dc in same st as join, dc in next st, 2 dc in next st, dc in next 26 sts, 3 dc in next st (**bottom point**), dc in next 26 sts, [2 dc in next st, dc in next 2 sts] 6 times, dc in next 21 sts, dc3tog (**center top**), dc in next 23 sts, 2 dc in next st, [dc in next 2 sts, 2 dc in next st] 4 times; join = 146 sts

Rnd 5: Ch 2, 2 dc in same st as join, dc in next 30 sts, 3 dc in next st (**bottom point**), dc in next 30 sts, 2 dc in next st, [dc in next 3 sts, 2 dc in next st] 5 times, dc in next 20 sts, dc3tog (**center top**), dc in next 20 sts, [2 dc in next st, dc in next 3 sts] 5 times; join = 158 sts

Rnd 6: Ch 2, dc in same st as join, dc in next 3 sts, 2 dc in next st, dc in next 28 sts, 3 dc in next st (**bottom point**), dc in next 28 sts, [2 dc in next st, dc in next 4 sts] 6 times, dc in next 19 sts, dc3tog (**center top**), dc in next 23 sts, 2 dc in next st, [dc in next 4 sts, 2 dc in next st] 4 times; join = 170 sts

Use stitch markers as you go to mark the **bottom point** and the **center top stitches.**

Rnd 7: Ch 2, 2 dc in same st as join, dc in next 34 sts, 3 dc in next st (**bottom point**), dc in next 34 sts, 2 dc in next st, [dc in next 5 sts, 2 dc in next st] 5 times, dc in next 18 sts, dc3tog (**center top**), dc in next 18 sts, [2 dc in next st, dc in next 5 sts] 5 times; join = 182 sts

Fasten off and weave in the ends. Block the muzzle if shaping is necessary (see General Techniques: Blocking).

MUZZLE CHART

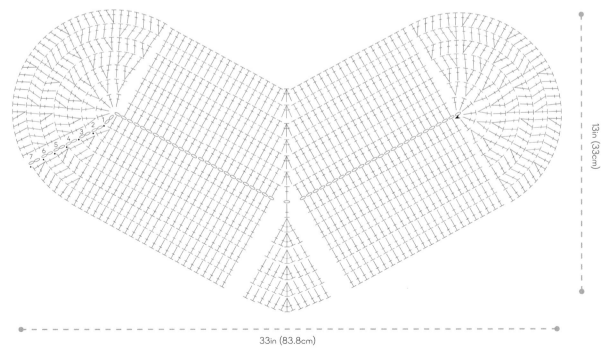

33in (83.8cm)

13in (33cm)

HORN CHART

7in (17.8cm)

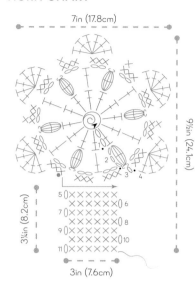

9½in (24.1cm)

3¼in (8.2cm)

3in (7.6cm)

EYE CHART

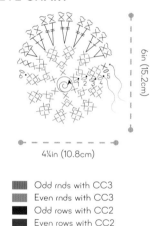

6in (15.2cm)

4¼in (10.8cm)

	Odd rnds with CC3
	Even rnds with CC3
	Odd rows with CC2
	Even rows with CC2

NOSTRIL CHART

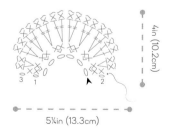

4in (10.2cm)

5¼in (13.3cm)

HORNS

Make 2. Begin by working in the round with a 9mm (M/N) hook and 3 strands of **CC1**.

To beg: Ch 3, sl st in third ch from hook to form a ring (or start with a magic ring)

Rnd 1: Ch 2 (does not count as a st) 12 dc in ring; join = 12 sts

Rnd 2: Beg PC in same st as join, ch 2, dc in next st, ch 2, [PC in next st, ch 2, dc in next st, ch 2] 5 times; join = 12 sts

Rnd 3: Ch 1 (does not count as a st now and throughout), skip beg PC, [3 sc in next ch-2 sp, skip st] 12 times; join = 36 sts

Rnd 4: Skip st with join, skip next st, 6 dc in next st, [skip 2 sts, sc in next st, skip 2 sts, 6 dc in next st] 4 times, skip 2 sts, sl st in next st = 5 shells

Continue to work in rows.

Rows 5-11: Ch 1, sc in next 6 sts; turn = 6 sts

Fasten off, leaving a long single strand of **CC1** for sewing. Weave in the other ends.

EYES

OUTER EYES

Make 2. Begin by working in the round with a 9mm (M/N) hook and 3 strands of **CC3**.

To beg: Ch 3, sl st in third ch from hook to form a ring (or start with a magic ring)

Rnd 1: Ch 1 (does not count as a st now and throughout), 6 sc in ring; join = 6 sts

Rnd 2: Ch 1, 2 sc in same st as join, 2 sc in next 5 sts; join = 12 sts

Rnd 3: Ch 1, 2 sc in same st as join, 2 sc in next 11 sts; join = 24 sts

Rnd 4: Ch 1, sc in same st as join, sc in next 23 sts; change to **CC2** and join = 24 sts

Break off **CC3**, leaving a long single strand for sewing. Continue to work in rows with **CC2**.

Row 5: (RS) Ch 1, skip st with join, sc in next st, 2 hdc in next st, 2 dc in next st, [2 tr in next st] 3 times, 2 dc in next st, 2 hdc in next st, sc in next st, sl st in next st; do not turn = 17 sts

Row 6: (RS) Ch 1, skip first sl st, rsc in next 15 sts, sl st in last st = 16 sts

Fasten off, leaving a long single strand of **CC2** for sewing. Weave in the other ends.

HIGHLIGHTS

Make 2 (see Common Shapes: Basic Eyes). Work with a 9mm (M/N) hook and 2 strands of **CC4**.

ASSEMBLING EYES

Place the highlights on top of the outer eyes and backstitch around, using the long tail from the highlight.

NOSTRILS

Make 2. Work in rows with a 9mm (M/N) hook and 2 strands of **CC2**.

To beg: Ch 7

Row 1: (WS) 2 sc in second ch from hook (the skipped ch does not count as a st), 2 sc in next 5 sts; turn = 12 sts

Row 2: (RS) Ch 1 (does not count as a st now and throughout), sc in first st, 2 hdc in next st, 2 dc in next st, 2 tr in next 6 sts, 2 dc in next st, 2 hdc in next st, sc in last st; do not turn = 22 sts

Row 3: (RS) Ch 1, skip first st, rsc in next 20 sts, sl st in last st = 21 sts

Fasten off, leaving a long single strand of **CC2** for sewing. Weave in the other ends.

BOW (OPTIONAL)

Make 1. Follow the instructions for the big bow (see Common Shapes: Big Bow). Use 3 strands of **CC5** with a 9mm (M/N) hook.

ASSEMBLING RUG

With RS facing, place the horns on the top of the head slightly under the head edge.

Place the muzzle to cover the bottom edge of the head.

Using the corresponding colors of yarn, backstitch across the overlapped edges of all pieces on RS (3).

Flip the rug to WS and whipstitch across the overlapped edges using the corresponding colors of yarn (4).

Position the eyes and the nostrils to create a facial expression (5).

Backstitch around the edge of each pupil using the long **CC3** tail and backstitch under the edge of the eyelids using the long **CC2** tail (6).

Using the long **CC2** tail from each nostril, backstitch below the rsc edge and whipstitch along the bottom edge (7).

If using, position the bow by the ear or under the muzzle and backstitch along the overlapping edge (8) or around the center.

If desired, make a removable non-slip lining (see General Techniques: Non-Slip Lining).

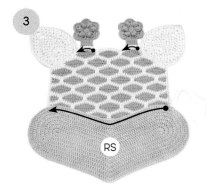

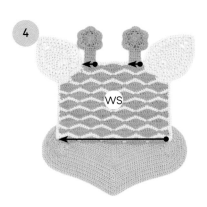

GIRAFFE PILLOW

SKILL LEVEL

FINISHED SIZE
14in x 20in (35.5cm x 50.8cm)

HOOKS
3.75mm (F), 4.25mm (G),
5mm (H), 5.5mm (I)

YARN WEIGHT
4

NUMBER OF STRANDS
1

**GAUGE WITH 1 STRAND
AND 5.5MM (I) HOOK**
14 sc x 16 rows = 4in x 4in (10cm x 10cm)

STITCH SUMMARY
Ch, sl st, sc, beg sc, sc2tog, rsc, hdc,
dc, dc3tog, tr, PC, beg PC, FDC, join

SKILLS
Working in rows and in the round,
raw edge finishing, working across
the bottom of the foundation chain,
changing colors, blocking, sewing

LEFT-HANDED CROCHET
See Crochet Techniques:
Left-Handed Crochet

YARN

Abbreviation	Color	Amount
CC5	Turquoise or Orange	350-415yd (320-380m)
CC6	Green and/or Orange	Small amount

All other colors are the same as for the
Giraffe Rug (small amount of each).

HEAD PILLOW BASE

Make 1 front and 1 back using 1 strand of **CC5** with a 5.5mm (I) hook. Follow the instructions for the oval pillow base (see Common Shapes: Oval Pillow Base). Fasten off after finishing each piece.

Holding the front and the back pieces together with WS facing each other, work the joining round through both pieces of fabric at the same time using a 5.5mm (I) hook and 1 strand of **CC6**.

Rnd 26: Beg sc in same st as previous sl st, sc in next 180 sts, stuff the pillow, sc in next 15 sts; join = 196 sts

Rnd 27: [Ch 3, 2 dc in same st, skip 2 sts, sl st in next st] 65 times = 65 points

Fasten off and weave in the ends.

HEAD

Make 1. Work in rows with a 5mm (H) hook and 1 strand of yarn, changing colors (**MC** and **CC1**) as indicated in the pattern.

NOTE: Ch-2 sps are not included in the total stitch count.

To beg: With **CC1**, ch 35

Row 1: (WS) Sc in second ch from hook (the skipped ch does not count as a st), hdc in next ch, dc in next 2 chs, tr in next 2 chs, dc in next 2 chs, hdc in next ch, sc in next ch, [ch 2, skip 2 chs, sc in next ch, hdc in next ch, dc in next 2 chs, tr in next 2 chs, dc in next 2 chs, hdc in next ch, sc in next ch] 2 times; change to **MC** and turn = 30 sts

HEAD CHART

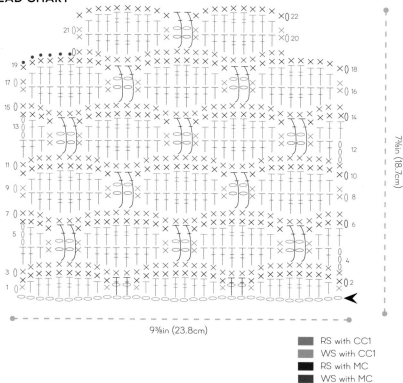

9⅜in (23.8cm)

7⅜in (18.7cm)

RS with CC1
WS with CC1
RS with MC
WS with MC

MUZZLE CHART

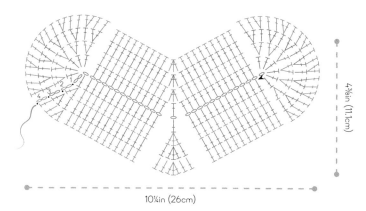

4⅜in (11.1cm)

10¼in (26cm)

Use stitch markers to mark the **bottom point** and the **center top** stitches of the muzzle.

Row 2: (RS) With **MC**, ch 1 (does not count as a st now and throughout), sc in first st, sc in next 9 sts, [dc in next 2 chs of the foundation row below, sc in next 10 sts] 2 times; turn = 34 sts

Row 3: (WS) Ch 1, sc in first st, sc in next 33 sts; change to **CC1** and turn = 34 sts

Row 4: (RS) With **CC1**, ch 3 (counts as first dc now and throughout), skip first st, dc in next st, hdc in next st, sc in next st, [ch 2, skip 2 sts, sc in next st, hdc in next st, dc in next 2 sts, tr in next 2 sts, dc in next 2 sts, hdc in next st, sc in next st] 2 times, ch 2, skip 2 sts, sc in next st, hdc in next st, dc in next 2 sts; turn = 28 sts

Row 5: (WS) Ch 3, skip first st, dc in next st, hdc in next st, sc in next st, [ch 2, skip ch-2 sp, sc in next st, hdc in next st, dc in next 2 sts, tr in next 2 sts, dc in next 2 sts, hdc in next st, sc in next st] 2 times, ch 2, skip ch-2 sp, sc in next st, hdc in next st, dc in next 2 sts; change to **MC** and turn = 28 sts

Row 6: (RS) With **MC**, ch 1, sc in first st, sc in next 3 sts, *[FDC in next sc two rows below] 2 times, skip ch-2 sp, sc in next 10 sts**, repeat 1 more time from * to **, [FDC in next sc two rows below] 2 times, skip ch-2 sp, sc in next 4 sts; turn = 34 sts

Row 7: (WS) Ch 1, sc in first st, sc in next 33 sts; change to **CC1** and turn = 34 sts

Row 8: (RS) With **CC1**, ch 1, sc in first st, hdc in next st, dc in next 2 sts, tr in next 2 sts, dc in next 2 sts, hdc in next st, sc in next st, [ch 2, skip 2 sts, sc in next st, hdc in next st, dc in next 2 sts, tr in next 2 sts, dc in next 2 sts, hdc in next st, sc in next st] 2 times; turn = 30 sts

Row 9: (WS) Ch 1, sc in first st, hdc in next st, dc in next 2 sts, tr in next 2 sts, dc in next 2 sts, hdc in next st, sc in next st, [ch 2, skip ch-2 sp, sc in next st, hdc in next st, dc in next 2 sts, tr in next 2 sts, dc in next 2 sts, hdc in next st, sc in next st] 2 times; change to **MC** and turn = 30 sts

Row 10: (RS) With **MC**, ch 1, sc in first st, sc in next 9 sts, *[FDC in next sc two rows below] 2 times, skip ch-2 sp, sc in next 10 sts**, repeat 1 more time from * to **; turn = 34 sts

Row 11: (WS) Ch 1, sc in first st, sc in next 33 sts; change to **CC1** and turn = 34 sts

Rows 12-17: Repeat Rows 4-9

Row 18: (RS) Repeat Row 10, carrying **CC1** across 6 sts at the beg of the row

Row 19: (WS) Sl st in first st, sl st in next 5 sts, ch 1, sc in next 22 sts; change to **CC1** and turn = 28 sts

Row 20: (RS) With **CC1**, ch 1, sc in first st, hdc in next st, dc in next 2 sts, tr in next 2 sts, dc in next 2 sts, hdc in next st, sc in next st, ch 2, skip 2 sts, sc in next st, hdc in next st, dc in next 2 sts, tr in next 2 sts, dc in next 2 sts, hdc in next st, sc in next st; turn = 20 sts

Row 21: (WS) Ch 1, sc in first st, hdc in next st, dc in next 2 sts, tr in next 2 sts, dc in next 2 sts, hdc in next st, sc in next st, ch 2, skip ch-2 sp, sc in next st, hdc in next st, dc in next 2 sts, tr in next 2 sts, dc in next 2 sts, hdc in next st, sc in next st; change to **MC**, break off **CC1** and turn = 20 sts

Row 22: (RS) With **MC**, ch 1, sc in first st, sc in next 9 sts, [FDC in next sc two rows below] 2 times, skip ch-2 sp, sc in next 10 sts = 22 sts

Fasten off and weave in the ends.

EDGING

With RS facing, begin working from the bottom right corner, using a 5.5mm (I) hook and 1 strand of **MC**.

Row 1: (RS) Beg sc, sc evenly around the edge towards the bottom left corner, placing 3 sc in each top corner for increasing. Do not work across the bottom edge and do not turn.

Row 2: (RS) Ch 1, rsc around the head towards the bottom right corner.

Fasten off, leaving a long tail for sewing. Wet block the head (see General Techniques: Blocking)

MUZZLE

Make 1. Work in the round with a 5mm (H) hook and 1 strand of **MC**.

To beg: Ch 29

Rnd 1: Dc in third ch from hook (2 skipped chs do not count as a st), dc in next 25 chs, 6 dc in last ch, continue working across the bottom of the foundation ch, dc in next 25 chs, 5 dc in last ch; join = 62 sts

Rnd 2: Ch 2 (does not count as a st now and throughout), 2 dc in same st as join, dc in next 12 sts, 3 dc in next st (**bottom point**), dc in next 12 sts, 2 dc in next 6 sts, dc in next 11 sts, dc3tog (**center top**), dc in next 11 sts, 2 dc in next 5 sts; join = 74 sts

Rnd 3: Ch 2, 2 dc in same st as join, dc in next 14 sts, 3 dc in next st (**bottom point**), dc in next 13 sts, [dc in next st, 2 dc in next st] 6 times, dc in next 10 sts, dc3tog (**center top**), dc in next 10 sts, [2 dc in next st, dc in next st] 5 times; join = 86 sts

Rnd 4: Ch 2, dc in same st as join, dc in next st, 2 dc in next st, dc in next 14 sts, 3 dc in next st (**bottom point**), dc in next 14 sts, [2 dc in next st, dc in next 2 sts] 6 times, dc in next 9 sts, dc3tog (**center top**), dc in next 9 sts, [dc in next 2 sts, 2 dc in next st] 5 times; join = 98 sts

Fasten off, leaving a long tail for sewing.

HORNS

Make 2. Begin by working in the round with a 5mm (H) hook and 1 strand of **CC1**.

To beg: Ch 3, sl st in third ch from hook to form a ring (or start with a magic ring)

Rnd 1: Ch 1 (does not count as a st now and throughout), 6 sc in ring; join = 6 sts

Rnd 2: Beg PC in same st as join, ch 2, [PC in next st, ch 2] 5 times; join = 6 sts

Rnd 3: Ch 1, skip beg PC, 3 sc in next ch-2 sp, [skip next PC, 3 sc in next ch-2 sp] 5 times; join = 18 sts

Rnd 4: [Ch 2, 2 dc in same st, skip st, sl st in next st] 7 times = 7 points

Continue to work in rows.

Row 5: Ch 1, sc in same st as previous sl st, sc in next 3 sts; turn = 4 sts

Rows 6-9: Ch 1, sc in each st across; turn = 4 sts

Fasten off, leaving a long tail for sewing.

EARS

Make 2. Work in spiral rounds with a 5.5mm (I) hook and 1 strand of **MC**.

Use a stitch marker to mark the beginning of each round as you go.

To beg: Ch 3, sl st in third ch from hook to form a ring (or start with a magic ring)

Rnd 1: Ch 1 (does not count as a st), 6 sc in ring; do not join now and throughout = 6 sts

Rnd 2: Sc in first st of previous rnd, sc in next 5 sts = 6 sts

Rnd 3: 2 sc in each st around = 12 sts

Rnd 4: Sc in each st around = 12 sts

Rnd 5: [Sc in next st, 2 sc in next st] 6 times = 18 sts

Rnd 6: Sc in each st around = 18 sts

Rnd 7: [Sc in next 2 sts, 2 sc in next st] 6 times = 24 sts

Rnd 8: Sc in each st around = 24 sts

Rnd 9: [Sc in next 3 sts, 2 sc in next st] 6 times = 30 sts

Rnds 10-16: Sc in each st around = 30 sts

Rnd 17: [Sc in next 3 sts, sc2tog] 6 times = 24 sts

Rnd 18: [Sc in next 2 sts, sc2tog] 6 times = 18 sts

Rnd 19: [Sc in next st, sc2tog] 6 times = 12 sts

Fasten off, leaving a long tail for sewing.

Holding the edge flat, whipstitch the opening; do not break off **MC**.

HORN CHART

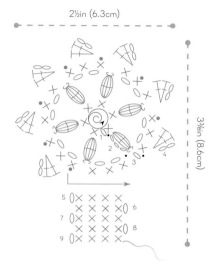

2½in (6.3cm)

3⅜in (8.6cm)

EYES

Make 2. Follow the instructions for the basic eyes (see Common Shapes: Basic Eyes). For the pupils, use 1 strand of **CC3** with a 4.25mm (G) hook and for the highlights use 1 strand of **CC4**.

BOW (OPTIONAL)

Make 1. Follow the instructions for the small bow (see Common Shapes: Small Bow). Use **CC6**.

ASSEMBLING PILLOW

Place the head onto the front of the pillow. Backstitch around the rsc edge and whipstitch across the straight bottom edge using the long **MC** tail from the head. Place the muzzle to cover the bottom edge of the head and backstitch around using the long **MC** tail from the muzzle (1).

Position the ears on each side of the head (2).

Using the long tail from each ear, whipstitch across the corresponding edge of the head, then bring the needle to the midpoint on the back side of the ear and whipstitch to secure (3 and 4).

Place the horns right up against the top of the head, evenly spaced between the ears and backstitch around using the long **CC1** tail from the horns (5).

Place the eyes on each side right up against the muzzle and backstitch around using the long **CC3** tail from the eyes (6).

A double-sided pillow would look just as adorable if you make the giraffes slightly different on each side. Finish both sides in the same manner; position the bow by the ear on one side and under the muzzle on the other side, and backstitch around the center of the bows.

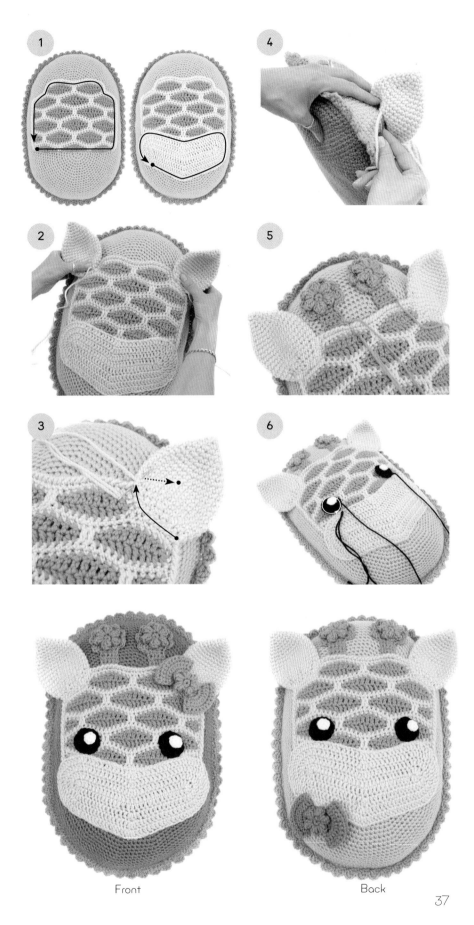

Front

Back

GIRAFFE SECURITY BLANKET

SKILL LEVEL

FINISHED SIZE
19½in x 19½in (49.5cm x 49.5cm)

HOOKS
3.75mm (F), 5mm (H)

YARN WEIGHT
4

NUMBER OF STRANDS
1

**GAUGE WITH 1 STRAND
AND 5MM (H) HOOK**
15 dc x 8 rows = 4in x 4in (10cm x 10cm)

STITCH SUMMARY
Ch, sl st, sc, sc2tog, bpsc, hdc,
dc, tr, FDC, picot, join

SKILLS
Working in rows and in the round,
raw edge finishing, working across
the bottom of the foundation chain,
changing colors, blocking, sewing

LEFT-HANDED CROCHET
Fully compatible

BLANKET

Make 1. Work in rows with a 5mm (H) hook and 1 strand of yarn, changing colors (**MC** and **CC1**) as indicated in the pattern.

NOTE: Ch-2 sps are not included in the total stitch count.

To beg: With **MC**, ch 71

Row 1: (WS) Sc in second ch from hook (the skipped ch does not count as a st), sc in next 69 chs; change to **CC1** and turn = 70 sts

Row 2: (RS) With **CC1**, ch 1 (does not count as a st now and throughout), sc in first st, hdc in next st, dc in next 2 sts, tr in next 2 sts, dc in next 2 sts, hdc in next st, sc in next st, [ch 2, skip 2 sts, sc in next st, hdc in next st, dc in next 2 sts, tr in next 2 sts, dc in next 2 sts, hdc in next st, sc in next st] 5 times; turn = 60 sts

YARN

Abbreviation	Color	Amount
MC	Yellow	208-240yd (190-220m)
CC1	Warm Brown	252-284yd (230-260m)
CC2	Coffee	Small amount

Row 3: (WS) Ch 1, sc in first st, hdc in next st, dc in next 2 sts, tr in next 2 sts, dc in next 2 sts, hdc in next st, sc in next st, [ch 2, skip ch-2 sp, sc in next st, hdc in next st, dc in next 2 sts, tr in next 2 sts, dc in next 2 sts, hdc in next st, sc in next st] 5 times; change to **MC** and turn = 60 sts

Row 4: (RS) With **MC**, ch 1, sc in first st, sc in next 9 sts, *[FDC in next sc two rows below] 2 times, skip ch-2 sp, sc in next 10 sts**, repeat 4 more times from * to **; turn = 70 sts

Row 5: (WS) Ch 1, sc in first st, sc in next 69 sts; change to **CC1** and turn = 70 sts

Row 6: (RS) With **CC1**, ch 3 (counts as first dc now and throughout), skip first st, dc in next st, hdc in next st, sc in next st, [ch 2, skip 2 sts, sc in next st, hdc in next st, dc in next 2 sts, tr in next 2 sts, dc in next 2 sts, hdc in next st, sc in next st] 5 times, ch 2, skip 2 sts, sc in next st, hdc in next st, dc in next 2 sts; turn = 58 sts

Row 7: (WS) Ch 3, skip first st, dc in next st, hdc in next st, sc in next st, [ch 2, skip ch-2 sp, sc in next st, hdc in next st, dc in next 2 sts, tr in next 2 sts, dc in next 2 sts, hdc in next st, sc in next st] 5 times, ch 2, skip ch-2 sp, sc in next st, hdc in next st, dc in next 2 sts; change to **MC** and turn = 58 sts

Row 8: (RS) With **MC**, ch 1, sc in first st, sc in next 3 sts, *[FDC in next sc two rows below] 2 times, skip ch-2 sp, sc in next 10 sts**, repeat 4 more times from * to **, [FDC in next sc two rows below] 2 times, skip ch-2 sp, sc in next 4 sts; turn = 70 sts

Row 9: (WS) Ch 1, sc in first st, sc in next 69 sts; change to **CC1** and turn = 70 sts

Rows 10-12: Repeat Rows 2-4

Rows 13-60: Repeat Rows 5-12 in established pattern until the blanket is visually square, ending after Row 12. Break off **CC1**.

BLANKET CHART

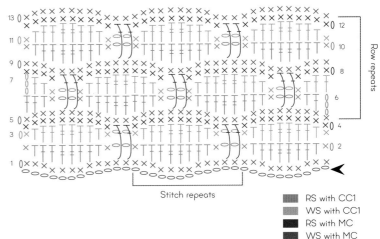

Stitch repeats

Row repeats

RS with CC1
WS with CC1
RS with MC
WS with MC

Edge: With **MC**, ch 1, *sc in next 2 sts, picot, repeat from * around, placing 3 sc in each corner for increasing; join

Fasten off and weave in the ends. Wet block the blanket (see General Techniques: Blocking).

HEAD

Make 1. Work in spiral rounds with a 3.75mm (F) hook and 1 strand of **MC**.

To beg: Ch 3, sl st in third ch from hook to form a ring (or start with a magic ring)

Rnd 1: Ch 1 (does not count as a st), 6 sc in ring; do not join now and throughout = 6 sts

Rnd 2: 2 sc in first st of previous rnd, 2 sc in next 4 sts, sc in next st = 11 sts

Rnd 3: 2 sc in each st around = 22 sts

Rnds 4-5: Sc in each st around = 22 sts

Rnd 6: [Sc in next st, 2 sc in next st] 11 times = 33 sts

Rnds 7-8: Sc in each st around = 33 sts

Rnd 9: [Sc in next 2 sts, 2 sc in next st] 11 times = 44 sts

Rnds 10-12: Sc in each st around = 44 sts

Use a stitch marker to mark the beginning of each round as you go.

Rnd 13: [Sc in next 3 sts, 2 sc in next st] 11 times = 55 sts

Rnds 14-18: Sc in each st around = 55 sts

Rnd 19: [Sc in next 3 sts, sc2tog] 11 times = 44 sts

Rnd 20: Sc in each st around = 44 sts

Rnd 21: [Sc in next 2 sts, sc2tog] 11 times = 33 sts

Rnd 22: Sc in each st around = 33 sts

Rnd 23: [Sc in next st, sc2tog] 11 times = 22 sts

Sl st in next st and fasten off, leaving a long tail for sewing. Stuff the head.

MUZZLE

Make 1. Work in spiral rounds with a 3.75mm (F) hook and 1 strand of **MC**.

To beg: Ch 5

Rnd 1: Sc in second ch from hook (the skipped ch does not count as a st), sc in next 2 chs, 3 sc in last ch, continue working across the bottom of the foundation ch, sc in next 2 chs, 2 sc in last ch; do not join now and throughout = 10 sts

Rnd 2: 2 sc in first st of previous rnd, sc in next 2 sts, 2 sc in next 3 sts, sc in next 2 sts, 2 sc in next 2 sts = 16 sts

Rnd 3: Sc in next st, 2 sc in next st, sc in next 2 sts, [sc in next st, 2 sc in next st] 3 times, sc in next 2 sts, [sc in next st, 2 sc in next st] 2 times = 22 sts

Rnd 4: 2 sc in next st, sc in next 4 sts, [2 sc in next st, sc in next 2 sts] 3 times, sc in next 2 sts, [2 sc in next st, sc in next 2 sts] 2 times = 28 sts

Rnds 5-6: Sc in each st around = 28 sts

Sl st in next st and fasten off, leaving a long tail for sewing.

Use a chopstick or a knitting needle for stuffing the horns.

HORNS

Make 2. Work in spiral rounds with a 3.75mm (F) hook and 1 strand of yarn, changing colors (**MC** and **CC1**) as indicated in the pattern.

To beg: With **CC1**, ch 3, sl st in third ch from hook to form a ring (or start with a magic ring)

Rnd 1: Ch 1 (does not count as a st), 6 sc in ring, do not join now and throughout = 6 sts

Rnd 2: 2 sc in first st of previous rnd, sc in next st, [2 sc in next st, sc in next st] 2 times = 9 sts

Rnds 3-4: Sc in each st around = 9 sts

Rnd 5: [Sc in next st, sc2tog] 3 times, change to **MC**, break off **CC1** = 6 sts

Rnd 6: With **MC**, sl st in next st, ch 1, sc in same st as sl st, sc in next 5 sts = 6 sts

Rnds 7-9: Sc in first st of previous rnd, sc in next 5 sts = 6 sts

Sl st in next st, fasten off, leaving a long tail for sewing. Stuff the horns.

EARS

Make 2 front and 2 back pieces. Work in rows with a 3.75mm (F) hook and 1 strand of **MC**.

To beg: Ch 6

Row 1: (RS) Sc in second ch from hook, sc in next ch, hdc in next 2 chs, 5 dc in last ch, continue working across the bottom of the foundation ch, hdc in next 2 chs, sc in next 2 chs = 13 sts

Fasten off after finishing each front piece, but do not break off yarn after finishing each back piece.

Place the front and the back pieces together with WS facing each other. Work the next row through both pieces of fabric at the same time using **MC** from the back piece.

Joining row: (RS) Ch 1, sc in next 6 sts, 3 sc in next st, sc in next 6 sts = 15 sts

Fasten off, leaving a long tail for sewing. Hide all the other ends inside of the ear using the tips of scissors or a chopstick.

ARMS

Make 2. Work in the round with a 3.75mm (F) hook and 1 strand of yarn, changing colors (**CC2** and **MC**) as indicated in the pattern. Stuff the arms as you go.

To beg: With **CC2**, ch 3, sl st in third ch from hook to form a ring (or start with a magic ring)

Rnd 1: Ch 1 (does not count as a st now and throughout), 6 sc in ring; join = 6 sts

Rnd 2: Ch 1, 2 sc in same st as join, 2 sc in next 5 sts; join = 12 sts

Rnd 3: Ch 1, 2 sc in same st as join, 2 sc in next 11 sts; join = 24 sts

Rnd 4: Ch 1, bpsc in same st as join, bpsc in next 23 sts; join = 24 sts

Rnd 5: Ch 1, sc in same st as join, sc in next st, sc2tog; [sc in next 2 sts, sc2tog] 5 times; join = 18 sts

Rnd 6: Ch 1, sc in same st as join, sc in next 17 sts; join = 18 sts

Rnd 7: Ch 1, sc in same st as join, sc2tog; [sc in next st, sc2tog] 5 times; join = 12 sts

Rnd 8: Ch 1, sc in same st as join, sc in next 11 sts; change to **MC**, break **CC2** = 12 sts

Rnd 9: With **MC**, ch 1, sc in same st as join, sc in next 11 sts; do not join now and throughout = 12 sts

Rnds 10-21: Sc in first st of previous rnd, sc in next 11 sts = 12 sts

Sl st in next st, fasten off, leaving a long tail for sewing. Holding the edge flat, whipstitch the opening and do not break off **MC**.

ASSEMBLING SECURITY BLANKET

Place the muzzle onto the head 2-3 rounds above the neck edge. Using the long **MC** tail from the muzzle, whipstitch around the edge leaving a small opening for stuffing. Stuff the muzzle and complete sewing (1).

Place the horns on the top of the head, one round apart from the center top and whipstitch around using the long **MC** tail from the horns. Place the ears on each side, right up against the horns and whipstitch around using the long **MC** tail from the ears (2).

Thread the needle with **CC1**. Chain stitch the smile, straight stitch the nostrils (3) and chain stitch the sleepy eyes (4).

Position the head in the center of the blanket and whipstitch around the neck edge using the long **MC** tail from the head.

Place the arms right up against the neck, facing both hooves in the same direction as the face. Whipstitch the arms around entire edge using the **MC** tail from the arms (5).

Prepare 3 groups of **MC** for the tail with 4 strands in each group, approximately 10in (25cm) long. Using a crochet hook, pull each bundle through the stitches on the back of the blanket and fold them in the middle. Braid the tail, then tie and trim the ends (6).

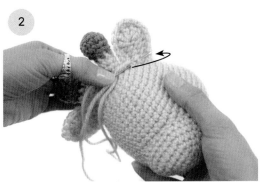

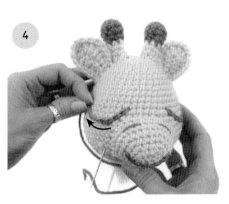

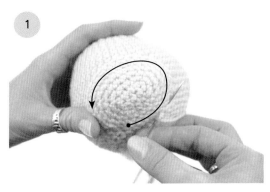

SASSY THE KITTY CAT

Rug, Pillow and Place Mat

Bring your granny square skills to the next level with this cute and fun kitty collection. Granny squares are never out of fashion because they are just so versatile! You can use a variety of colored yarns to create interesting patterns or simplify the design by just using one or two shades.

Sassy was inspired by a traditional granny square motif that was adapted into a heart shape. I love the bold contrast between black cat and pastel colors in the heart as they create a beautiful modern appearance. However, you may chose to soften the look by using lighter colors for your kitty and hand stitch sleepy eyes.

KITTY RUG

SKILL LEVEL

FINISHED SIZE
48in x 40in (122cm x 101.6cm)

HOOKS
5.5mm (I), 9mm (M/N)

YARN WEIGHT
4

NUMBER OF STRANDS
1, 2 and 3

GAUGE WITH 3 STRANDS AND 9MM (M/N) HOOK
9 dc x 4.5 rows = 4in x 4in (10cm x 10cm)

STITCH SUMMARY
Ch, sl st, sc, sc2tog, rsc, hdc, dc, dc2tog, tr, picot, PC, beg PC, crest, cluster, shell, arch, join

SKILLS
Working in rows and in the round, working across the bottom of the foundation chain, changing colors, blocking, sewing

LEFT-HANDED CROCHET
See Crochet Techniques: Left-Handed Crochet

YARN

Abbreviation	Color	Amount
MC	Black or Gray	1039–1148yd (950–1050m)
CC1	Any leftover yarn in a variety of colors or a solid color yarn	1203–1312yd (1100–1200m)
CC2	Pink	93–109yd (85–100m)
CC3	Black	Small amount
CC4	White	Small amount
CC5	Blue or Green	Small amount
CC6	Burgundy (optional)	93–109yd (85–100m)

HEART

Make 1. Begin by working in the round with a 9mm (M/N) hook and 3 strands of **CC1**. Change colors in any round or use a solid color yarn for the entire heart.

> Use stitch markers as you go to mark the **bottom point and center top**.

STEP 1 - SET-UP

To beg: Ch 33

Set-up row: (RS) 3 dc in sixth ch from hook (5 skipped chs count as first dc plus ch 2), [skip 2 chs, 3 dc in next ch] 8 times, skip 2 chs, dc in last ch = 9 clusters and 2 dc

Do not turn. Continue to work **Step 2** around the set-up row on RS.

STEP 2 - HEART

Rnd 1: (Ch 3, 2 dc) in same end sp (counts as beg cluster now and throughout), [ch 3, 3 dc in same end sp] 2 times, continue working across the bottom of the foundation ch [skip cluster, 3 dc in next ch-2 sp between clusters] 8 times, 3 dc in next ch-5 sp, [ch 3, 3 dc in same end sp] 2 times, continue working across the top of the set-up row [skip cluster, 3 dc in next sp between clusters] 3 times, skip cluster, dc next 3 sts of the cluster, [skip cluster, 3 dc in next sp between clusters] 3 times; sl st in top of beg ch-3 = 20 clusters and 3 dc

HEART CHART

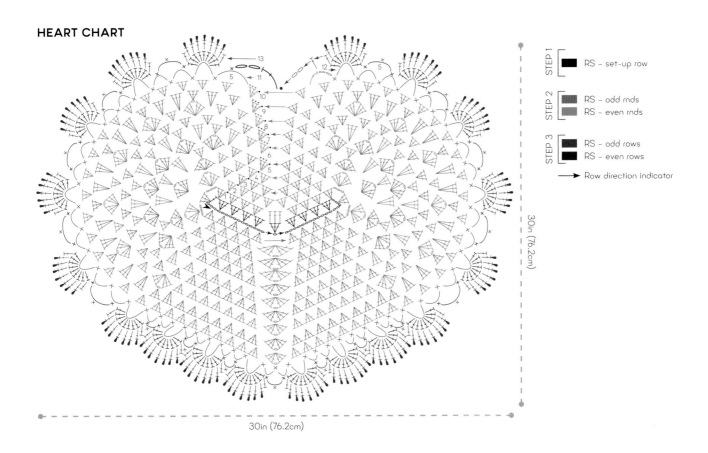

30in (76.2cm)

30in (76.2cm)

STEP 1 ■ RS – set-up row

STEP 2 ▨ RS – odd rnds
▨ RS – even rnds

STEP 3 ▨ RS – odd rows
■ RS – even rows

→ Row direction indicator

Rnd 2: (Ch 3, 2 dc) in same sp between clusters, [skip cluster, (3 dc, ch 1, 3 dc) in next arch] 2 times, [skip cluster, 3 dc in next sp between clusters] 4 times, skip cluster, (3 dc, ch 1, 3 dc) in next sp between clusters (**bottom point**), [skip cluster, 3 dc in next sp between clusters] 4 times, [skip cluster, (3 dc, ch 1, 3 dc) in next arch] 2 times, [skip cluster, 3 dc in next sp between clusters] 4 times, skip 3 dc (**center top**), [3 dc in next sp between clusters, skip cluster] 3 times; sl st in top of beg ch-3 = 26 clusters

Rnd 3: (Ch 3, 2 dc) in same sp between clusters, skip cluster, 3 dc in next sp between clusters, [skip cluster, (3 dc, ch 1, 3 dc) in next sp between clusters] 3 times, [skip cluster, 3 dc in next sp between clusters] 5 times, skip cluster, (3 dc, ch 1, 3 dc) in next sp between clusters (**bottom point**), [skip cluster, 3 dc in next sp between clusters] 5 times, [skip cluster, (3 dc, ch 1, 3 dc) in next sp between clusters] 3 times, [skip cluster, 3 dc in next sp between clusters] 4 times, skip 2 clusters (**center top**), [3 dc in next sp between clusters, skip cluster] 2 times; sl st in top of beg ch-3 = 32 clusters

Rnd 4: (Ch 3, 2 dc) in same sp between clusters, [skip cluster, 3 dc in next sp between clusters] 13 times, skip cluster, (3 dc, ch 1, 3 dc) in next sp between clusters (**bottom point**), [skip cluster, 3 dc in next sp between clusters] 15 times, skip 2 clusters (**center top**), 3 dc in next sp between clusters; sl st in top of beg ch-3 = 32 clusters

Rnd 5: (Ch 3, 2 dc) in same sp between clusters, [skip cluster, 3 dc in next sp between clusters] 2 times, [skip cluster, (3 dc, ch 1, 3 dc) in next sp between clusters] 6 times, [skip cluster, 3 dc in next sp between clusters] 6 times, skip cluster, (3 dc, ch 1, 3 dc) in next sp between clusters (**bottom point**), [skip cluster, 3 dc in next sp between clusters] 6 times, [skip cluster, (3 dc, ch 1, 3 dc) in next sp between clusters] 6 times, [skip cluster, 3 dc in next sp between clusters] 3 times, skip 2 clusters (**center top**); sl st in top of beg ch-3 = 44 clusters

Rnds 6-7: Sl st in next 2 dc, sl st in sp between clusters, (ch 3, 2 dc) in same sp, [skip cluster, 3 dc in next sp between clusters] 20 times, skip cluster, (3 dc, ch 1, 3 dc) in next sp between clusters (**bottom point**), [skip cluster, 3 dc in next sp between clusters] 21 times, skip 2 clusters (**center top**); sl st in top of beg ch-3 = 44 clusters

Rnd 8: Sl st in next 2 dc, sl st in sp between clusters, (ch 3, 2 dc) in same sp, skip cluster, 3 dc in next sp between clusters, *skip cluster, 3 dc in next sp between clusters, skip cluster, (3 dc, ch 1, 3 dc) in next sp between clusters**, repeat 5 more times from * to **, [skip cluster, 3 dc in next sp between clusters] 7 times, skip cluster, (3 dc, ch 1, 3 dc) in next sp between clusters (**bottom point**), [skip cluster, 3 dc in next sp between clusters] 6 times, repeat 6 times from * to **, [skip cluster, 3 dc in next sp between clusters] 3 times, skip 2 clusters (**center top**); sl st in top of beg ch-3 = 56 clusters

Rnd 9: Sl st in next 2 dc, sl st in sp between clusters, (ch 3, 2 dc) in same sp, [skip cluster, 3 dc in next sp between clusters] 26 times, skip cluster, (3 dc, ch 1, 3 dc) in next sp between clusters (**bottom point**), [skip cluster, 3 dc in next sp between clusters] 27 times, skip 2 clusters (**center top**); sl st in top of beg ch-3 = 56 clusters

Rnd 10: Sl st in next 2 dc, sl st in sp between clusters, (ch 3, 2 dc) in same sp, [skip cluster, 3 dc in next sp between clusters] 26 times, skip cluster, (3 dc, ch 1, 3 dc) in next sp between clusters (**bottom point**), [skip cluster, 3 dc in next sp between clusters] 27 times, skip 2 clusters (**center top**); sl st in top of beg ch-3, sl st in next 2 dc; sl st in sp between clusters = 56 clusters

Do not break off yarn. Continue to work **Step 3** in rows, beginning on RS.

STEP 3 - EDGING

Row 11: (RS) [Ch 5, skip cluster, sc in next sp between clusters] 53 times, skip cluster, ch 2, dc in next sp between clusters (counts as last arch); turn = 54 arches

Row 12: (WS) Skip ch-2 sp, [9 dc in next arch, sc in next arch, ch 5, sc in next arch] 17 times, 9 dc in next arch, sc in next arch, skip next cluster of Rnd 10, ch 2, dc in next sp between clusters (counts as last arch); turn = 18 shells and 18 arches

Row 13: (RS) Skip ch-2 sp, [crest across next shell, sc in next arch] 17 times, crest across next shell, dc in last dc of Row 11, ch 2, skip next cluster of Rnd 10; sl st in sp between clusters (**center top**) = 18 crests

Fasten off and weave in the ends. Spray block the heart to enhance the finished look of the lace texture (see General Techniques: Blocking).

HEAD CHART

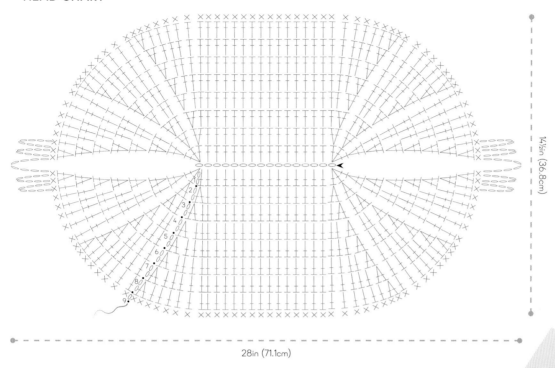

14½in (36.8cm)

28in (71.1cm)

HEAD

Make 1. Work in the round with a 9mm (M/N) hook and 3 strands of **MC**.

To beg: Ch 18

Rnd 1: Dc in third ch from hook (2 skipped chs do not count as a st), dc in next 14 chs, 6 dc in last ch, continue working across the bottom of the foundation ch, dc in next 14 chs, 5 dc in last ch; join = 40 sts

Rnd 2: Ch 2 (does not count as a st now and throughout), 2 dc in same st as join, dc in next 14 sts, 2 dc in next 6 sts, dc in next 14 sts, 2 dc in next 5 sts; join = 52 sts

Rnd 3: Ch 2, 2 dc in same st as join, dc in next 16 sts, [2 dc in next st, dc in next st] 2 times, 2 dc in next 2 sts, [dc in next st, 2 dc in next st] 2 times, dc in next 16 sts, [2 dc in next st, dc in next st] 2 times, 2 dc in next st, [2 dc in next st, dc in next st] 2 times; join = 64 sts

Rnd 4: Ch 2, 2 dc in same st as join, dc in next 18 sts, [2 dc in next st, dc in next 2 sts] 2 times, 2 dc in next 2 sts, [dc in next 2 sts, 2 dc in next st] 2 times, dc in next 18 sts, [2 dc in next st, dc in next 2 sts] 2 times, 2 dc in next st, [2 dc in next st, dc in next 2 sts] 2 times; join = 76 sts

Rnd 5: Ch 2, 2 dc in same st as join, dc in next 20 sts, [2 dc in next st, dc in next 3 sts] 2 times, 2 dc in next 2 sts, [dc in next 3 sts, 2 dc in next st] 2 times, dc in next 20 sts, [2 dc in next st, dc in next 3 sts] 2 times, 2 dc in next st, [2 dc in next st, dc in next 3 sts] 2 times; join = 88 sts

Rnd 6: Ch 2, 2 dc in same st as join, dc in next 22 sts, [2 dc in next st, dc in next 4 sts] 2 times, 2 dc in next 2 sts, [dc in next 4 sts, 2 dc in next st] 2 times, dc in next 22 sts, [2 dc in next st, dc in next 4 sts] 2 times, 2 dc in next st, [2 dc in next st, dc in next 4 sts] 2 times; join = 100 sts

Blocking will help to achieve a symmetrical appearance.

Rnd 7: Ch 2, 2 dc in same st as join, dc in next 24 sts, [2 dc in next st, dc in next 5 sts] 2 times, 2 dc in next 2 sts, [dc in next 5 sts, 2 dc in next st] 2 times, dc in next 24 sts, [2 dc in next st, dc in next 5 sts] 2 times, 2 dc in next st, [2 dc in next st, dc in next 5 sts] 2 times; join = 112 sts

Rnd 8: Ch 2, 2 dc in same st as join, dc in next 26 sts, [2 dc in next st, dc in next 6 sts] 2 times, 2 dc in next 2 sts, [dc in next 6 sts, 2 dc in next st] 2 times, dc in next 26 sts, [2 dc in next st, dc in next 6 sts] 2 times, 2 dc in next st, [2 dc in next st, dc in next 6 sts] 2 times; join = 124 sts

Rnd 9: Ch 1 (does not count as a st), sc in same st as join, sc in next 43 sts, [ch 8, sc in next st] 5 times, sc in next 57 sts, [ch 8, sc in next st] 5 times, sc in next 13 sts; join = 124 sts and 5 loops on each side of the head

Fasten off, leaving a long single strand of **MC** for sewing. Weave in the other ends. Block the head if shaping is necessary (see General Techniques: Blocking).

EARS

Make 2. Work in rows with a 9mm (M/N) hook and 3 strands of yarn, changing colors (**CC2** and **MC**) as indicated in the pattern.

To beg: With **CC2**, ch 2

Row 1: (WS) 3 sc in second ch from hook (the skipped ch does not count as a st); turn = 3 sts

Row 2: (RS) Ch 1 (does not count as a st now and throughout), 2 sc in first st, 3 sc in next st, 2 sc in last st; turn = 7 sts

Row 3: (WS) Ch 1, 2 sc in first st, sc in next 2 sts, 3 sc in next st, sc in next 2 sts, 2 sc in last st; turn = 11 sts

Row 4: (RS) Ch 1, 2 sc in first st, sc in next 4 sts, 3 sc in next st, sc in next 4 sts, 2 sc in last st; turn = 15 sts

Row 5: (WS) Ch 1, 2 sc in first st, sc in next 6 sts, 3 sc in next st, sc in next 6 sts, 2 sc in last st, change to **MC** and break off **CC2**; turn = 19 sts

Row 6: (RS) With **MC**, ch 1, 2 sc in first st, sc in next 8 sts, 3 sc in next st, sc in next 8 sts, 2 sc in last st; do not turn = 23 sts

Row 7: (RS) Ch 1, skip first st, rsc in next 21 sts; sl st in last st = 22 sts

Fasten off, leaving a long single strand of **MC** for sewing. Weave in the other ends.

NOSE

Make 1. Work in the round with a 5.5mm (I) hook and 1 strand of **CC2**.

To beg: Ch 6

Rnd 1: Sc in second ch from hook (the skipped ch does not count as a st), sc in next 3 chs, 3 sc in last ch, continue working across the bottom of the foundation ch, sc in next 3 chs, 2 sc in last ch; join = 12 sts

Rnd 2: Ch 1 (does not count as a st), 2 sc in same st as join, sc in next 3 sts, 2 sc in next 3 sts, skip st, (hdc, dc, hdc) in next st, skip st, 2 sc in next 2 sts; join = 18 sts

Fasten off, leaving a long tail for sewing.

EYES

Make 2. Each eye includes a basic eye, an iris and an outer eye.

BASIC EYES

Make 2. Follow the instructions for the basic eyes (see Common Shapes: Basic Eyes). Work with a 5.5mm (I) hook using 1 strand of **CC3** for the pupils and 1 strand of **CC4** for the highlights.

IRISES

Make 2. Work in the round with a 5.5mm (I) hook and 1 strand of **CC5**.

To beg: Ch 3, sl st in third ch from hook to form a ring (or start with a magic ring)

Rnd 1: Ch 2 (does not count as a st), 12 dc in ring; join = 12 sts

Rnd 2: Ch 1 (does not count as a st now and throughout), 2 sc in same st as join, 2 sc in next 3 sts, skip st, (hdc, dc, tr) in next st, (tr, dc, hdc) in next st, skip st, 2 sc in next 4 sts; join = 22 sts

Rnd 3: Ch 1, sc in same st as join, sc in next 9 sts, 2 sc in next 2 sts, sc in next 10 sts; join = 24 sts

Fasten off, leaving a long tail for sewing.

EAR CHART

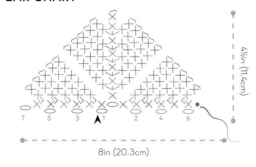

8in (20.3cm)

4½in (11.4cm)

NOSE CHART

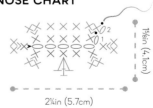

2¼in (5.7cm)

1⅝in (4.1cm)

OUTER EYES

Make 2. Work in the round with a 5.5mm (I) hook and 1 strand of **CC4**.

To beg: Ch 3, sl st in third ch from hook to form a ring (or start with a magic ring)

Rnd 1: Ch 2 (does not count as a st now and throughout), 12 dc in ring; join = 12 sts

Rnd 2: Ch 2, 2 dc in same st as join, 2 dc in next 11 sts; join = 24 sts

Rnd 3: Ch 1 (does not count as a st now and throughout), sc in same st as join, 2 sc in next st, [sc in next st, 2 sc in next st] 4 times, skip st, (hdc, dc, tr) in next st, (tr, dc, hdc) in next st, skip st, [sc in next st, 2 sc in next st] 5 times; join = 36 sts

Rnd 4: Ch 1, sc in same st as join, sc in next 16 sts, 2 sc in next 2 sts, sc in next 17 sts; join = 38 sts

Fasten off, leaving a long tail for sewing.

ASSEMBLING EYES

Place the basic eye on top of the iris and backstitch around using the long **CC3** tail from the pupil. Then place the iris on top of the outer eye and backstitch around using the long **CC5** tail from the iris (1). Finish the second eye in the same manner.

IRIS CHART

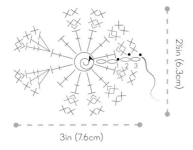

2½in (6.3cm)

3in (7.6cm)

OUTER EYE CHART

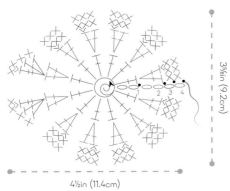

3⅝in (9.2cm)

4½in (11.4cm)

Line up all pieces as close to the pointy edges as possible.

1

PAWS

Make 4. Work in the round with a 9mm (M/N) hook and 3 strands of **MC**.

To beg: Ch 7

Rnd 1: Dc in third ch from hook (2 skipped chs do not count as a st), dc in next 3 chs, 6 dc in last ch, continue working across the bottom of the foundation ch, dc in next 3 chs, 5 dc in last ch; join = 18 sts

Rnd 2: Ch 2 (does not count as a st now and throughout), 2 dc in same st as join, dc in next 3 sts, 2 dc in next 6 sts, dc in next 3 sts, 2 dc in next 5 sts; join = 30 sts

Rnd 3: Ch 2, dc in same st as join, 2 dc in next st, dc in next 3 sts, [dc in next st, 2 dc in next st] 6 times, dc in next 3 sts, [dc in next st, 2 dc in next st] 5 times; join = 42 sts

Rnd 4: Ch 1 (does not count as a st), sc in same st as join, sc in next st, 2 sc in next st, sc in next 5 sts, 2 sc in next st, [sc in next 2 sts, 2 sc in next st] 2 times, *sc in next st, skip st, 6 dc in next st, skip st**, [sc in next st, skip 2 sts, 6 dc in next st, skip 2 sts] 2 times, repeat from * to **, sc in next 3 sts, 2 sc in next st, sc in next 2 sts, 2 sc in next st; join = 32 sc and 4 shells

Fasten off and weave in the ends.

> **Make 2 paws with pads and 2 paws without pads.**

PAW PADS

Make 2 sets. Each set includes 1 palm pad and 4 toe pads. Work in the round with a 9mm (M/N) hook and 2 strands of **CC2**.

TOE PADS

To beg: Ch 3, sl st in third ch from hook to form a ring (or start with a magic ring)

Rnd 1: Ch 1 (does not count as a st), 6 sc in ring; join = 6 sts

Fasten off, leaving a long single strand of **CC2** for sewing. Weave in the other ends.

PALM PADS

To beg: Ch 7

Rnd 1: Dc in third ch from hook (2 skipped chs do not count as a st), dc in next 3 chs, 6 dc in last ch, continuing working across the bottom of the foundation ch, dc in next 3 chs, 5 dc in next ch; join = 18 sts

Rnd 2: Ch 1 (does not count as a st), 2 sc in same st as join, sc in next 3 sts, 2 sc in next 5 sts, skip 2 sts, 6 dc in next st, skip 2 sts, 2 sc in next 4 sts; join = 23 sc and 1 shell

Fasten off, leaving a long single strand of **CC2** for sewing. Weave in the other ends.

ASSEMBLING PAWS

With RS facing, place the first set of paw pads on top of the first paw and backstitch around the edge using the long tail from each piece (2). Finish the second paw in the same manner. The remaining 2 paws do not need paw pads.

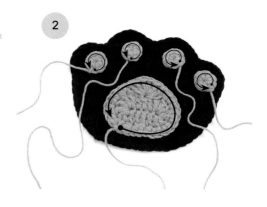

PAW CHART

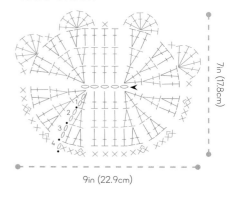

7in (17.8cm)

9in (22.9cm)

PAW PAD CHART

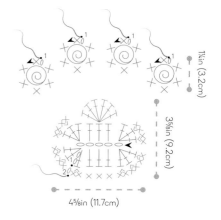

1¼in (3.2cm)

3⅝in (9.2cm)

4⅝in (11.7cm)

Use solid colors for the heart to create a different look.

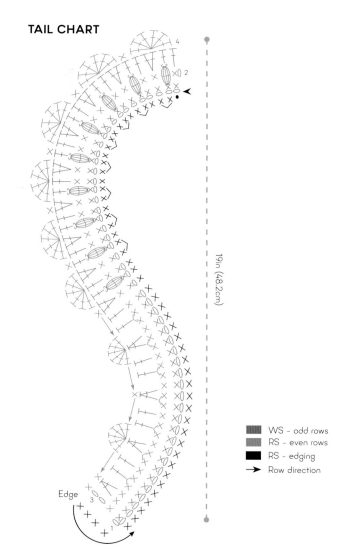

3

Finish

Begin

TAIL CHART

WS - odd rows
RS - even rows
RS - edging
→ Row direction

Edge

19in (48.2cm)

TAIL

Make 1. Work in rows with a 9mm (M/N) hook and 3 strands of **MC.**

To beg: Ch 52

Row 1: (WS) Sc in second ch from hook (the skipped ch does not count as a st), sc in next 50 chs; turn = 51 sts

Row 2: (RS) Ch 1 (does not count as a st now and throughout), sc in first st, [PC in next st, sc in next 2 sts] 9 times, [sc2tog, sc in next st] 7 times, sc in next 2 sts; turn = 9 PC and 35 sc

Row 3: (WS) Ch 2 (counts as first dc), skip first st, [dc2tog, dc in next 2 sts] 4 times, [2 dc in next st, dc in next 2 sts] 9 times; turn = 49 sts

Row 4: (RS) [Skip 2 sts, 6 dc in next st, skip 2 sts, sc in next st] 8 times, sc in last st = 8 shells and 9 sc

Do not break off yarn, but rotate your work and continue to work edging.

Edge: (RS) 4 sc evenly across the side sts of the tail, continue working across the bottom of the foundation ch, sc in next 27 sts, [sc2tog, sc in next st] 7 times, sc2tog; sl st in last st = 43 sts

Fasten off and weave in the ends (3).

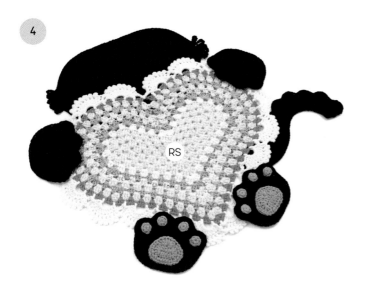

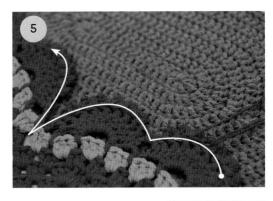

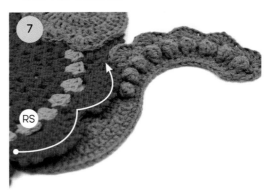

BOW (OPTIONAL)

Make 1. Follow the instructions for the big bow (see Common Shapes: Big Bow). Use 3 strands of **CC6** with a 9mm (M/N) hook.

ASSEMBLING RUG

With RS facing, cover the bottom part of the head with the top edge of the heart (4).

Place 2 paws without pads on each side of the heart below the head, covering the scalloped edge. Place the remaining 2 paws at the bottom of the heart, covering the scalloped edge. All paws should be extending beyond the heart edge (4).

Place a portion of the tail under the scalloped edge of the heart (4).

Using the corresponding colors of yarn, backstitch across the overlapped edges of all pieces on RS (5-7).

Flip the rug to WS and whipstitch across the overlapped edges using the corresponding colors of yarn (8).

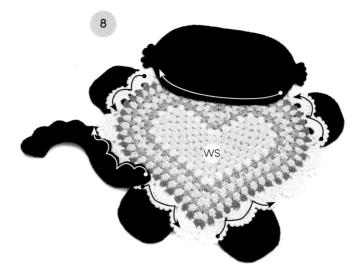

Place the eyes, nose and ears onto the head to create your chosen facial expression. Backstitch around the eyes using the long **CC4** tail from the outer eyes (9). Backstitch around the nose using the long **CC2** tail from the nose, then chain stitch a few stitches down from the center of the nose (10).

Using the long **MC** tail from the ears, whipstitch across the edges on RS and WS (11).

Position the bow (if using) and backstitch around the center of the bow using **CC6** (12). Keep the side edges of the bow unattached or whipstitch the corners if you would like to keep them in place.

If desired, make a removable non-slip lining (see General Techniques: Non-Slip Lining).

Create an adorable look by placing a bow on the heart instead.

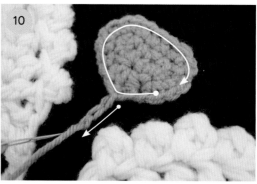

KITTY PILLOW

SKILL LEVEL

FINISHED SIZE
25in x 15½in (63.5cm x 39.4cm)
including edging

HOOKS
5.5mm (I), 9mm (M/N)

YARN WEIGHT
4

NUMBER OF STRANDS
1 and 3

GAUGE WITH 1 STRAND
AND 5.5MM (I) HOOK
14 sc x 16 rows = 4in x 4in (10cm x 10cm)

STITCH SUMMARY
Ch, sl st, sc, sc3tog, rsc, hdc,
dc, PC, beg PC, join

SKILLS
Working in rows and in the round,
working across the bottom of
the foundation chain, sewing

LEFT-HANDED CROCHET
Fully compatible

YARN

Abbreviation	Color	Amount
MC	Black or Gray	547-569yd (500-520m)

Other contrasting colors are the same as for the
Kitty Rug except CC1 (small amount of each).

HEAD PILLOW BASE

Make 1 front and 1 back using 1 strand of MC with a 5.5mm (I) hook. Follow the instructions for the oval pillow base (see Common Shapes: Oval Pillow Base). Fasten off after finishing the back piece, but do not break off yarn after finishing the front piece.

Fold the front piece in half horizontally and mark 6 stitches on each side for whiskers by placing a marker in first and sixth stitches. Holding the front and the back pieces together with WS facing each other, work the joining round through both pieces of fabric at the same time using the working yarn from the front piece. Remove markers as you go.

Rnd 26: Ch 1 (does not count as a st), sc in same st as previous sl st, sc in each st towards the next marker, *sc in st with marker, [ch 20, sc in next st] 5 times (ending in st with next marker)**, sc in each st towards the next marker, stuff the pillow (1), repeat from * to **, sc in each st towards the beg st; join = 196 sts and 5 loops on each side

Fasten off and weave in the ends.

EYES

Make 2 for kitty with opened eyes. Follow the instructions for the eyes from the Kitty Rug (see Kitty Rug: Eyes). Work with a 5.5mm (I) hook using 1 strand of **CC3** for the pupils, 1 strand of **CC4** for the highlights, 1 strand of **CC5** for the irises and 1 strand of **CC4** for the outer eyes.

NOSE

Make 1. Follow the instructions for the nose from the Kitty Rug (see Kitty Rug: Nose). Work with a 5.5mm (I) hook and 1 strand of **CC2**.

EARS

Make 2. Follow the instructions for the ears from the Kitty Rug (see Kitty Rug: Ears). Work with a 9mm (M/N) hook and 3 strands of yarn, changing colors (**CC2** and **MC**) as indicated in the pattern.

BOW (OPTIONAL)

Make 1. Working with **CC6**, follow the instructions for the big bow (see Common Shapes: Big Bow) or small bow (see Common Shapes: Small Bow).

ASSEMBLING PILLOW

Place the nose below the center of the pillow base and backstitch around using the long **CC2** tail from the nose, then chain stitch a few stitches down from the center of the nose (2).

Stuff

Place the eyes on each side of the nose and backstitch around using the long **CC4** tail from the eyes (2) or chain stitch sleepy eyes using **CC3** (3).

Place the ears on each side of the head, 3-4 rounds below the joining round. Use clips or stitch markers to hold the ears in place while sewing. Do not use straight basting pins as they can easily get lost in the pillow.

Using the long MC tail from the ears, whipstitch twice around the entire edge (4 and 5).

Place the bow onto the head and backstitch around the center using the long **CC6** tail from the bow (6).

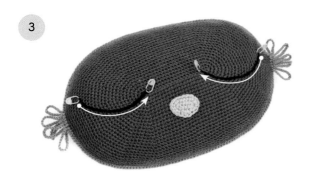

Simply chain stitch eyes for the sleepy kitty.

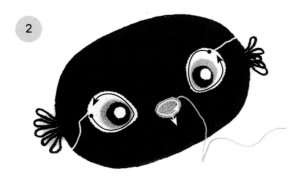

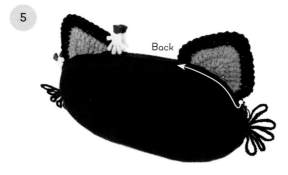

KITTY PLACE MAT

SKILL LEVEL

FINISHED SIZE

Place mat: 15½in-10in (39.4cm-25.4cm)

Coaster: 5¼in-4¼in (13.3cm-10.8cm)

HOOKS

3.75mm (F), 5mm (H)

YARN WEIGHT

4

NUMBER OF STRANDS

1

GAUGE WITH 1 STRAND AND 5MM (H) HOOK

15 dc x 8 rows = 4in x 4in (10cm x 10cm)

STITCH SUMMARY

Ch, sl st, sc, rsc, hdc, dc, join

SKILLS

Working in rows and in the round, working across the bottom of the foundation chain, sewing

LEFT-HANDED CROCHET

Fully compatible

YARN

Abbreviation	Color	Amount
MC	Black or Gray	148-180yd (135-165m)

Other contrasting colors are the same as for the Kitty Rug except **CC1** (small amount of each).

PLACE MAT

HEAD

Make 1. Follow the instructions for the head from the Kitty Rug (see Kitty Rug: Head). Work with a 5mm (H) hook and 1 strand of **MC**.

EYES

Make 2 for kitty with opened eyes. Follow the instructions for the eyes from the Kitty Rug (see Kitty Rug: Eyes). Work with a 3.75mm (F) hook using 1 strand of **CC3** for the pupils, 1 strand of **CC4** for the highlights, 1 strand of **CC5** for the irises and 1 strand of **CC4** for the outer eyes.

NOSE

Make 1. Follow the instructions for the nose from the Kitty Rug (see Kitty Rug: Nose). Work with a 3.75mm (F) hook and 1 strand of **CC2**.

EARS

Make 2. Follow the instructions for the ears from the Kitty Rug (see Kitty Rug: Ears). Work with a 5mm (H) hook and 1 strand of yarn, changing colors (**CC3** and **MC**) as indicated in the pattern.

ASSEMBLING PLACE MAT

Place the eyes, nose and ears onto the head to create a facial expression. Backstitch the eyes using the long **CC4** tail from the eyes (1) or chain stitch sleepy eyes using **CC3** (2).

Backstitch the nose using the long **CC2** tail from the nose and chain stitch a few stitches down from the center of the nose (1). Whipstitch the ears around entire edge using **MC** tail from the ears.

PAW COASTERS

Make 2. Follow the instructions for the paws from the Kitty Rug (see Kitty Rug: Paws). Work with a 5mm (H) hook and 1 strand of **MC**.

Block your finished pieces if shaping is necessary.

ROCK 'N' ROLL PANDA

Rug, Pillow and Toy Bag

Pandas are the cutest bears in the world and they never hibernate, which means they rock all year round! They love rolling in the grass and chewing on bamboo sticks. What a fun way to spend a day.

This pattern collection was created for the love of pandas inspired by our eldest daughter Amanda. Just like pandas, she is cute and cuddly but when agitated, watch out!!

You can make a playful panda with a star patch, or just use oval patches for a classic panda look.

PANDA RUG

SKILL LEVEL

 ○ ○

FINISHED SIZE
42in x 32in (106.7cm x 81.3cm)

HOOK
9mm (M/N)

YARN WEIGHT
4

NUMBER OF STRANDS
3

**GAUGE WITH 3 STRANDS
AND 9MM (M/N) HOOK**
9 dc x 4.5 rows = 4in x 4in (10cm x 10cm)

STITCH SUMMARY
Ch, sl st, sc, rsc, hdc, dc, tr,
dc2tog, PC, shell, join

SKILLS
Working in rows and in the round, raw
edge finishing, working across the
bottom of the foundation chain, sewing

LEFT-HANDED CROCHET
Fully compatible

YARN

Abbreviation	Color	Amount
MC	White	1011-1202yd (925-1100m)
CC1	Black	612-656yd (560-600m)
CC2	Lush Green	459-546yd (420-500m)
CC3	Red (optional)	93-109yd (85-100m)

HEAD

Make 1. Work in the round with a 9mm (M/N) hook and 3 strands of **MC**.

To beg: Ch 3, sl st in third ch from hook to form a ring (or start with a magic ring)

Rnd 1: Ch 2 (does not count as a st now and throughout), 12 dc in ring; join = 12 sts

Rnd 2: Ch 2, 2 dc in same st as join, 2 dc in next 11 sts; join = 24 sts

Rnd 3: Ch 2, dc in same st as join, 2 dc in next st, [dc in next st, 2 dc in next st] 11 times; join = 36 sts

Rnd 4: Ch 2, 2 dc in same st as join, dc in next 2 sts, [2 dc in next st, dc in next 2 sts] 11 times; join = 48 sts

Rnd 5: Ch 2, dc in same st as join, dc in next 2 sts, 2 dc in next st, [dc in next 3 sts, 2 dc in next st] 11 times; join = 60 sts

Rnd 6: Ch 2, 2 dc in same st as join, dc in next 4 sts, [2 dc in next st, dc in next 4 sts] 11 times; join = 72 sts

Rnd 7: Ch 2, dc in same st as join, dc in next 4 sts, 2 dc in next st, [dc in next 5 sts, 2 dc in next st] 11 times; join = 84 sts

Rnd 8: Ch 2, 2 dc in same st as join, dc in next 6 sts, [2 dc in next st, dc in next 6 sts] 11 times; join = 96 sts

Rnd 9: Ch 2, dc in same st as join, dc in next 6 sts, 2 dc in next st, [dc in next 7 sts, 2 dc in next st] 11 times; join = 108 sts

Rnd 10: Ch 2, 2 dc in same st as join, dc in next 8 sts, [2 dc in next st, dc in next 8 sts] 11 times; join = 120 sts

Rnd 11: Ch 2, dc in same st as join, dc in next 8 sts, 2 dc in next st, [dc in next 9 sts, 2 dc in next st] 11 times; join = 132 sts

Rnd 12: Ch 2, 2 dc in same st as join, dc in next 10 sts, [2 dc in next st, dc in next 10 sts] 11 times; join = 144 sts

Rnd 13: Ch 2, dc in same st as join, dc in next 10 sts, 2 dc in next st, [dc in next 11 sts, 2 dc in next st] 11 times; join = 156 sts

Rnd 14: Ch 2, 2 dc in same st as join, dc in next 12 sts, [2 dc in next st, dc in next 12 sts] 11 times; join = 168 sts

Rnd 15: Ch 2, dc in same st as join, dc in next 12 sts, 2 dc in next st, [dc in next 13 sts, 2 dc in next st] 11 times; join = 180 sts

Rnd 16: Ch 2, 2 dc in same st as join, dc in next 14 sts, [2 dc in next st, dc in next 14 sts] 11 times; join = 192 sts

Fasten off and weave in the ends.

HEAD CHART

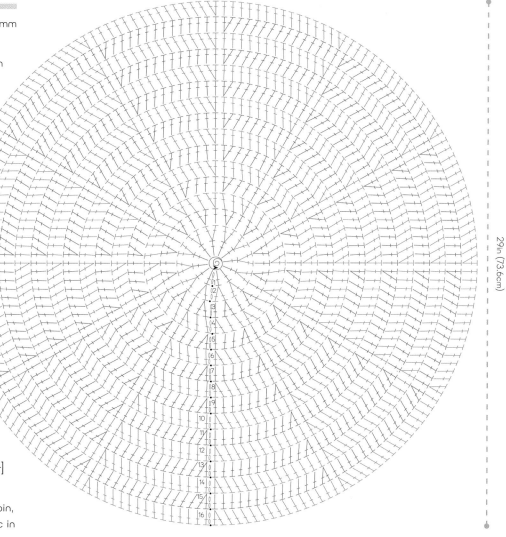

29in (73.6cm)

EAR CHART

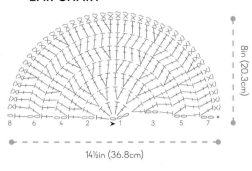

14½in (36.8cm)

8in (20.3cm)

NOSE CHART

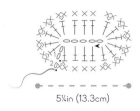

5¼in (13.3cm)

OVAL PATCH CHART

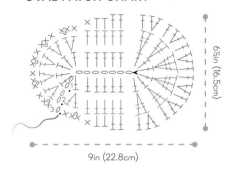

9in (22.8cm)

6½in (16.5cm)

EARS

Make 2. Work in rows with a 9mm (M/N) hook and 3 strands of **CC1**.

To beg: Ch 3

Row 1: (RS) 5 dc in third ch from hook (2 skipped chs count as first dc); turn = 6 sts

Row 2: (WS) Ch 2 (counts as first dc now and throughout), dc in first st, 2 dc in next 5 sts; turn = 12 sts

Row 3: (RS) Ch 2, dc in first st, dc in next st, [2 dc in next st, dc in next st] 5 times; turn = 18 sts

Row 4: (WS) Ch 2, dc in first st, dc in next 2 sts, [2 dc in next st, dc in next 2 sts] 5 times; turn = 24 sts

Row 5: (RS) Ch 2, dc in first st, dc in next 3 sts, [2 dc in next st, dc in next 3 sts] 5 times; turn = 30 sts

Row 6: (WS) Ch 2, dc in first st, dc in next 4 sts, [2 dc in next st, dc in next 4 sts] 5 times; turn = 36 sts

Row 7: (RS) Ch 2, dc in first st, dc in next 5 sts, [2 dc in next st, dc in next 5 sts] 5 times; do not turn = 42 sts

Row 8: (RS) Ch 1 (does not count as a st), skip first st, rsc in next 40 sts, sl st in last st = 41 sts

Fasten off and weave in the ends.

NOSE

Make 1. Work in the round with a 9mm (M/N) hook and 3 strands of **CC1**.

To beg: Ch 7

Rnd 1: Dc in third ch from hook (2 skipped chs do not count as a st), dc in next 3 chs, 6 dc in last ch, continue working across the bottom of the foundation ch, dc in next 3 chs, 5 dc in last ch; join = 18 sts

Rnd 2: Ch 1 (does not count as a st), 2 sc in same st as join, sc in next 3 sts, 2 sc in next 6 sts, sc in next 3 sts, 2 sc in next 5 sts; join = 30 sts

Fasten off, leaving a long single strand of **CC1** for sewing. Weave in the other ends.

EYE PATCHES

Make 1 oval patch and 1 star patch or 2 oval patches for a classic panda look. Work in the round with a 9mm (M/N) hook and 3 strands of **CC1**.

OVAL PATCH

To beg: Ch 9

Rnd 1: Dc in third ch from hook (2 skipped chs do not count as a st), dc in next 5 chs, 6 dc in last ch, continue working across the bottom of the foundation ch, dc in next 5 chs, 5 dc in last ch; join = 22 sts

Rnd 2: Ch 2 (does not count as a st), 2 dc in same st as join, dc in next 5 sts, 2 tr in next 2 sts, 3 tr in next 2 sts, 2 tr in next 2 sts, dc in next 5 sts, 2 dc in next 5 sts; join = 36 sts

Rnd 3: Ch 1 (does not count as a st), sc in same st as join, 2 sc in next st, sc in next st, hdc in next 2 sts, dc in next 3 sts, [2 dc in next st, dc in next st] 3 times, [dc in next st, 2 dc in next st] 3 times, dc in next 3 sts, hdc in next 2 sts, sc in next st, [sc in next st, 2 sc in next st] 5 times; join = 48 sts

Fasten off, leaving a long single strand of **CC1** for sewing. Weave in the other ends.

STAR PATCH CHART

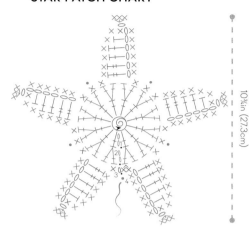

10¾in (27.3cm)

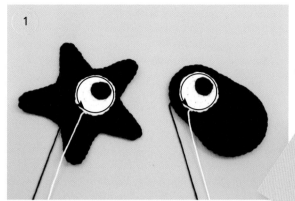

Make 2 matching oval patches for a classic panda look.

STAR PATCH

To beg: Ch 3, sl st in third ch from hook to form a ring (or start with a magic ring)

Rnd 1: Ch 2 (does not count as a st now and throughout), 12 dc in ring; join = 12 sts

Rnd 2: Ch 2, 2 dc in same st as join, 2 dc in next 11 sts; join = 24 sts

Rnd 3: Ch 1 (does not count as a st), 2 sc in same st as join, ch 7, sc in second ch from hook, hdc in next ch, dc in next 2 chs, tr in next 2 chs (first point made), *skip 2 sts of previous rnd, sc in next 3 sts, ch 7, sc in second ch from hook, hdc in next ch, dc in next 2 chs, tr in next 2 chs (next point made)**, repeat 3 more times from * to **, skip 2 sts of previous rnd, sc in next st; join = 5 points and 15 sc

Rnd 4: Skip st with join, *skip next st, sc across next 6 foundation sts of the point, 3 sc in last ch of the point, sc in next 6 sts of the point, skip next st, sl st in next st**, repeat 4 more times from * to ** = 80 sts

Fasten off, leaving a long single strand of **CC1** for sewing. Weave in the other ends.

EYES

Make 2 outer eyes with a 9mm (M/N) hook and 3 strands of **MC**, following the instructions for pupils (see Common Shapes: Basic Eyes). Make 2 pupils with a 9mm (M/N) hook and 3 strands of **CC1**, following the instructions for highlights, then assemble the eyes (see Common Shapes: Basic Eyes) (1).

BAMBOO

Make 1. Work in rows with a 9mm (M/N) hook and 3 strands of **CC2**.

To beg: Ch 15

Row 1: (RS) Dc in fourth ch from hook (3 skipped chs count as first dc), dc in next 11 chs; turn = 13 sts

Rows 2-7: Ch 2 (counts as first dc now and throughout), skip first st, dc in next 12 sts; turn = 13 sts

Row 8: (WS) Ch 2, dc in first st, dc in next 11 sts, 2 dc in last st; turn = 15 sts

Row 9: (RS) Ch 2, skip first st, [PC in next st, dc in next st] 7 times; turn = 15 sts

BAMBOO CHART

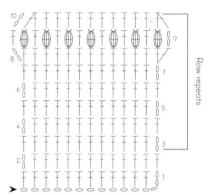

Row repeats

Row 10: (WS) Ch 2, skip first st, dc2tog, dc in next 10 sts, dc2tog; turn = 13 sts

Rows 11-34: Repeat Rows 3-10 in established pattern, ending on WS

Rows 35-41: Ch 2, skip first st, dc in next 12 sts; turn = 13 sts

Edge: (RS) Ch 1, sc evenly around entire edge, placing 3 sc in each corner for increasing; join

Fasten off and weave in ends.

PAWS

Make 2. Follow the instructions for the paws in the Kitty Rug (see Kitty Rug: Paws). Work with a 9mm (M/N) hook and 3 strands of **CC1**.

BOW (OPTIONAL)

Make 1. Follow the instructions for the big bow using **CC3** (see Common Shapes: Big Bow).

ASSEMBLING RUG

With RS facing, position the nose 4 rounds below the center of the head. Position the oval patch 4 rounds away from the center of the head. Position the star patch 5 rounds away from the center of the head. Place the bamboo to cover 5-7 bottom rounds of the head (2).

Using the corresponding colors of yarn, backstitch around the eyes, around the nose and across the overlapped edge of the bamboo.

With RS facing, place the ears slightly under the head edge, positioning them symmetrically on each side of the head with approximately 38 stitches between the ears (3).

Backstitch across the overlapped edge of the head using **MC**.

Position the paws diagonally on each side of the head, covering the edges of the head and the bamboo (3).

Backstitch across the overlapped edges of the paws using **CC1** (3).

Flip the rug to WS and whipstitch across the overlapped edges using the corresponding colors of yarn (4).

If using, place the bow onto the head and backstitch around the center with **CC3** (5).

Keep the side edges of the bow unattached or whipstitch the corners if you would like to keep them in place.

If desired, make a removable non-slip lining (see General Techniques: Non-Slip Lining).

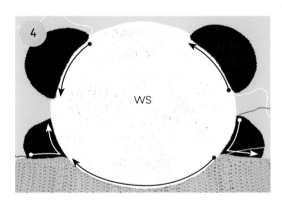

PANDA PILLOW

SKILL LEVEL

FINISHED SIZE
17in x 14½in (43.2cm x 36.8cm)

HOOKS
4.25mm (G), 5.5mm (I), 9mm (M/N)

YARN WEIGHT
4

NUMBER OF STRANDS
1 and 3

**GAUGE WITH 1 STRAND
AND 5.5MM (I) HOOK**
14 sc x 16 rows = 4in x 4in (10cm x 10cm)

STITCH SUMMARY
Ch, sl st, sc, rsc, hdc, dc, tr, join

SKILLS
Working in rows and in the round,
working across the bottom of
the foundation chain, sewing

LEFT-HANDED CROCHET
Fully compatible

YARN

Abbreviation	Color	Amount
MC	White	120-164yd (110-150m)
CC1	Black	109-120yd (100-110m)
CC2	Red (optional)	93-109yd (85-100m)
CC3	Variegated Red	120-164yd (110-150m)

HEAD PILLOW BASE

Make 1 front using 1 strand of **MC** and 1 back using 1 strand
of **CC3** with a 5.5mm (I) hook. Follow the instructions for
the round pillow base (see Common Shapes: Round Pillow
Base). Fasten off after finishing the back piece, but do not
break off yarn after finishing the front piece.

Holding the front and the back pieces together with WS
facing each other, work the joining round through both
pieces of fabric at the same time, using the working yarn
from the front piece.

Rnd 26: Ch 1 (does not count as a st), sc in same st as
previous sl st, sc in next 140 sts, stuff the pillow, sc in next
15 sts; join = 156 sts

Fasten off and weave in the ends.

EARS

Make 2. Follow the instructions for the ears in the Panda Rug from the beginning to Row 3 (see Panda Rug: Ears). Use a 9mm (M/N) hook and 3 strands of **CC1**. Continue to work the last row as follows:

Row 4: (RS) Ch 1 (does not count as a st), skip first st, rsc in next 16 sts, sl st in last st = 17 sts

Fasten off, leaving a long tail for sewing.

NOSE

Make 1. Follow the instructions for the nose in the Panda Rug, omitting the last round (see Panda Rug: Nose). Work with a 4.25mm (G) hook and 1 strand of **CC1**.

EYE PATCHES

Make 1 oval patch and 1 star patch, or 2 oval patches for a classic panda look. Follow the instructions for the eye patches in the Panda Rug (see Panda Rug: Eye Patches). Work with a 4.25mm (G) hook and 1 strand of **CC1**.

EYES

Make 2 outer eyes with a 4.25mm (G) hook and 1 strand of **MC**, following the instructions for pupils (see Common Shapes: Basic Eyes). Make 2 pupils with a 4.25mm (G) hook and 1 strand of **CC1**, following the instructions for highlights, then assemble the eyes (see Common Shapes: Basic Eyes). Place the eyes on top of the eye patches and backstitch around using **MC**.

BOW (OPTIONAL)

Make 1. Follow the instructions for the big bow using **CC2** (see Common Shapes: Big Bow).

ASSEMBLING PILLOW

Position the nose 6 rounds below the center on the front side of the pillow base. Position the oval patch 6 rounds away from the center. Position the star patch 7 rounds away from the center (1).

Backstitch around each piece using **CC1**.

Place the ears on each side of the head, 3-4 rounds below the joining round. Use clips or stitch markers to hold the ears in place while sewing. Using **CC1**, whipstitch the ears twice around entire edge, removing clips as you sew (2 and 3).

If using, place the bow onto the head and backstitch around the center using **CC2** (4).

Avoid using pins as they may get lost in the pillow.

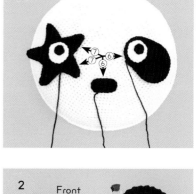

1

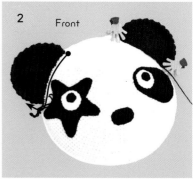

2 Front

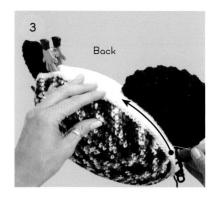

3 Back

4

PANDA TOY BAG

SKILL LEVEL

FINISHED SIZE
18½in x 35in (47cm x 88.9cm)

HOOKS
3.75mm (F), 5.5mm (I), 9mm (M/N)

YARN WEIGHT
4

NUMBER OF STRANDS
1, 2 and 3

**GAUGE WITH 2 STRANDS
AND 9MM (M/N) HOOK**
10 dc x 5 rows = 4in x 4in (10cm x 10cm)

STITCH SUMMARY
Ch, sl st, sc, rsc, hdc, dc, tr, join

SKILLS
Working in rows and in the
round, working across the
bottom of the foundation chain,
changing colors, sewing

LEFT-HANDED CROCHET
Fully compatible

YARN

Abbreviation	Color	Amount
MC	White	93-109yd (85-100m)
CC1	Black	93-109yd (85-100m)
CC2	Lush Green	93-109yd (85-100m)
CC3	Red (optional)	Small amount
CC4	Variegated Red	1312-1531yd (1200-1400m)

TOY BAG

Make 1. Work in the round with a 9mm (M/N) hook and 2 strands of **CC4**.

To beg: Ch 45

Rnd 1: Dc in third ch from hook (2 skipped chs do not count as a st), dc in next 42 chs, 3 dc in last ch, continue working across the bottom of the foundation ch, dc in next 42 chs, 2 dc in last ch; join = 90 sts

Rnds 2–38: Ch 2 (does not count as a st), dc in same st as join, dc in next 89 sts; join = 90 sts

Break off **CC4**, join **CC2** and continue to work the edge:

Edge: Ch 1 (does not count as a st), sc in same st as join, sc in next 5 sts, *ch 10, sl st in second ch from hook, sc in next ch, hdc in next ch, dc in next 3 chs, hdc in next ch, sc in next 2 chs (leaf made)**, [sc in next 6 sts of previous rnd, repeat from * to ** for next leaf] 14 times; join = 15 leaves and 90 sc

Fasten off and weave in the ends.

DRAWSTRING

Make 1. Work with a 9mm (M/N) hook and 3 strands of **CC2**.

To beg: Ch 150

Fasten off and trim the ends. Using a crochet hook, pull the drawstring around the post of the center stitch 4 rounds below the edge and tie a knot to secure the drawstring. Thread each end of the drawstring through the stitches of the same round (1).

HEAD

Make 1. Follow the instructions for the head in the Panda Rug pattern from the beginning to Rnd 9 (see Panda Rug: Head). Use a 5.5mm (I) hook and 1 strand of **MC**. Continue to work the last round as follows:

Rnd 10: Ch 1 (does not count as a st), sc in same st as join, sc in next 107 sts; join = 108 sts

Fasten off, leaving a long tail for sewing.

EARS

Make 2. Follow the instructions for the ears in the Panda Rug from the beginning to Row 5 (see Panda Rug: Ears). Use a 5.5mm (I) hook and 1 strand of **CC1**. Continue to work the last row as follows:

Row 6: (RS) Ch 1 (does not count as a st), skip first st, rsc in next 28 sts, sl st in last st = 29 sts

Fasten off, leaving a long tail for sewing.

NOSE

Make 1. Follow the nose instructions in the Panda Rug, omitting the last round (see Panda Rug: Nose). Work with a 3.75mm (F) hook and 1 strand of **CC1**.

EYE PATCHES

Make 1 oval patch and 1 star patch, or 2 oval patches for a classic panda look. Work with a 3.75mm (F) hook and 1 strand of **CC1**.

OVAL PATCH

Follow the oval patch instructions in the Panda Rug, omitting the last round (see Panda Rug: Eye Patches).

STAR PATCH CHART

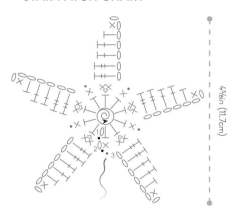

4⅝in (11.7cm)

STAR PATCH

To beg: Ch 3, sl st in third ch from hook to form a ring (or start with a magic ring)

Rnd 1: Ch 1 (does not count as a st now and throughout), 10 hdc in ring; join = 10 sts

Rnd 2: Ch 1, sc in same st as join, 2 sc in next st, [sc in next st, 2 sc in next st] 4 times; join = 15 sts

Rnd 3: Ch 7, sc in second ch from hook, hdc in next ch, dc in next 2 chs, tr in next 2 chs (first point made), skip st with join, skip next 2 sts, sl st in next st, *ch 7, sc in second ch from hook, hdc in next ch, dc in next 2 chs, tr in next 2 chs (next point made), skip 2 sts, sl st in next st**, repeat 3 more times from * to ** = 5 points

Fasten off, leaving a long tail for sewing.

EYES

Make 2 outer eyes with a 3.75mm (F) hook and 1 strand of **MC**, following the instructions for pupils (see Common Shapes: Basic Eyes). Make 2 pupils with a 3.75mm (F) hook and 1 strand of **CC1**, following the instructions for highlights, then assemble the eyes (see Common Shapes: Basic Eyes). Place the eyes on top of the eye patches and backstitch around using **MC**.

BOW (OPTIONAL)

Make 1. Follow the instructions for the big bow using **CC3** (see Common Shapes: Big Bow).

ASSEMBLING TOY BAG

With RS facing, position the nose and the eyes 2 rounds away from the center of the head and backstitch around each piece with **CC1** (2).

Place the ears slightly under the head edge, positioning them symmetrically on each side of the head with approximately 18 stitches between the ears (2). Backstitch across the overlapped edge of the head using **MC**.

Position the head in the middle of the bag. Backstitch around the head edge using the **MC** and backstitch around the outer edges of the ears using **CC1** (3).

If using, place the bow onto the head and backstitch around the center using **CC3** (4).

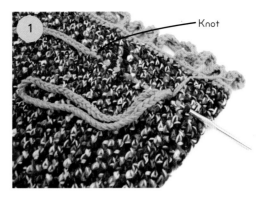

CHIP THE MONKEY

Rug, Pillow and Toy Bag

This chapter is all about monkey business. If you enjoy crocheting for your little monkeys, here are a few ideas to keep them monkeying around. At the end of a long day in the jungle, cleaning up is a lot easier if you have a cheerful toy bag to help motivate your troop, who can look forward to a snuggly reading time with a cute monkey pillow on a matching reading rug when the job is done.

There is no better time to teach crafts to the next generation; as you know, monkey see - monkey do! You might even enjoy crocheting together!

MONKEY RUG

SKILL LEVEL

FINISHED SIZE
36in x 35in (91.4cm x 88.9cm)

HOOK
Hook 9mm (M/N)

YARN WEIGHT
4

NUMBER OF STRANDS
3

GAUGE WITH 3 STRANDS AND 9MM (M/N) HOOK
9 dc x 4.5 rows = 4in x 4in (10cm x 10cm)

STITCH SUMMARY
Ch, sl st, sc, sc2tog, fpsc, rsc, hdc, dc, dc2tog, slipknot, join

SKILLS
Working in rows and in the round, raw edge finishing, working across the bottom of the foundation chain, changing colors, sewing

LEFT-HANDED CROCHET
See Crochet Techniques: Left-Handed Crochet

YARN

Abbreviation	Color	Amount
MC	Beige	710-820yd (650-750m)
CC1	Coffee	360-437yd (330-400m)
CC2	Yellow	710-820yd (650-750m)
CC3	Warm Brown	Small amount
CC4	Any color (optional)	93-109yd (85-100m)

HEAD

Make 1. Work in rows with a 9mm (M/N) hook and 3 strands of **CC1**.

To beg: Ch 8

Row 1: (WS) Dc in fourth ch from hook (3 skipped chs count as dc), dc in next 3 chs, 6 dc in last ch, continue working across the bottom of the foundation ch, dc in next 5 chs; turn = 16 sts

Row 2: (RS) Ch 2 (counts as first dc now and throughout), skip first st, dc in next 4 sts, 2 dc in next 6 sts, dc in next 5 sts; turn = 22 sts

Row 3: (WS) Ch 2, skip first st, dc in next 4 sts, [2 dc in next st, dc in next st] 6 times, dc in next 5 sts; turn = 28 sts

Row 4: (RS) Ch 2, skip first st, dc in next 4 sts, [2 dc in next st, dc in next 2 sts] 6 times, dc in next 5 sts; turn = 34 sts

Row 5: (WS) Ch 2, skip first st, dc in next 4 sts, [2 dc in next st, dc in next 3 sts] 6 times, dc in next 5 sts; turn = 40 sts

Row 6: (RS) Ch 2, skip first st, dc in next 4 sts, [2 dc in next st, dc in next 4 sts] 6 times, dc in next 5 sts; turn = 46 sts

Row 7: (WS) Ch 2, skip first st, dc in next 4 sts, [2 dc in next st, dc in next 5 sts] 6 times, dc in next 5 sts; turn = 52 sts

Row 8: (RS) Ch 2, skip first st, dc in next 4 sts, [2 dc in next st, dc in next 6 sts] 6 times, dc in next 5 sts; turn = 58 sts

Row 9: (WS) Ch 2, skip first st, dc in next 4 sts, [2 dc in next st, dc in next 7 sts] 6 times, dc in next 5 sts; turn = 64 sts

HEAD CHART

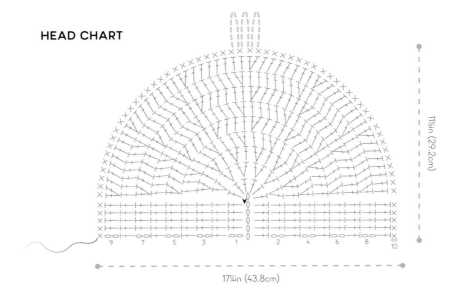

11½in (29.2cm)

17¼in (43.8cm)

Row 10: (RS) Ch 1 (does not count as a st), sc in first st, sc in next 30 sts, [ch 10, sc in next st] 3 times, sc in next 30 sts = 64 sc and 3 ch-10 loops

Fasten off, leaving a long single strand of **CC1** for sewing. Weave in the other ends.

EARS

Make 2. Work in rows with a 9mm (M/N) hook and 3 strands of yarn, changing colors (**MC** and **CC1**) as indicated in the pattern.

To beg: With **MC**, ch 3

Row 1: (WS) 5 dc in third ch from hook (2 skipped chs count as dc); turn = 6 sts

Row 2: (RS) Ch 2 (counts as first dc now and throughout), dc in first st, 2 dc in next 5 sts; turn = 12 sts

Row 3: (WS) Ch 2, dc in first st, dc in next st, [2 dc in next st, dc in next st] 5 times, change to **CC1** and break off **MC**; turn = 18 sts

EAR CHART

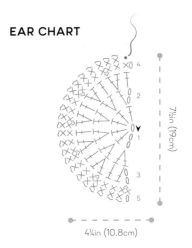

7½in (19cm)

4¼in (10.8cm)

Row 4: (RS) With **CC1**, ch 1 (does not count as a st now and throughout), sc in first st, sc in next st, 2 sc in next st, [sc in next 2 sts, 2 sc in next st] 5 times; do not turn = 24 sts

Row 5: (RS) Ch 1, skip first st, rsc in next 22 sts, sl st in last st = 23 sts

Fasten off, leaving a long single strand of **CC1** for sewing. Weave in the other ends.

MUZZLE

Make 1. Work in the round with a 9mm (M/N) hook and 3 strands of **MC**.

To beg: Ch 32

Rnd 1: Dc in third ch from hook (2 skipped chs do not count as a st), dc in next 28 chs, 6 dc in last ch, continue working across the bottom of the foundation ch, dc in next 28 chs, 5 dc in last ch; join = 68 sts

Rnd 2: Ch 2 (does not count as a st now and throughout), 2 dc in same st as join, dc in next 28 sts, 2 dc in next 6 sts, dc in next 28 sts, 2 dc in next 5 sts; join = 80 sts

Rnd 3: Ch 2, dc in same st as join, 2 dc in next st, dc in next 28 sts, [dc in next st, 2 dc in next st] 6 times, dc in next 28 sts, [dc in next st, 2 dc in next st] 5 times; join = 92 sts

Rnd 4: Ch 2, 2 dc in same st as join, dc in next 30 sts, [2 dc in next st, dc in next 2 sts] 6 times, dc in next 28 sts, [2 dc in next st, dc in next 2 sts] 5 times; join = 104 sts

Rnd 5: Ch 2, dc in same st as join, dc in next 2 sts, 2 dc in next st, dc in next 28 sts, [dc in next 3 sts, 2 dc in next st] 6 times, dc in next 28 sts, [dc in next 3 sts, 2 dc in next st] 5 times; join = 116 sts

Rnd 6: Ch 2, 2 dc in same st as join, dc in next 32 sts, [2 dc in next st, dc in next 4 sts] 6 times, dc in next 28 sts, [2 dc in next st, dc in next 4 sts] 5 times; join = 128 sts

Fasten off and weave in the ends.

SMILE

With RS of the muzzle facing, mark the bottom half of Rnd 2 for the smile (40 stitches).

Work around the marked stitches with a 9mm (M/N) hook and 3 strands of **CC1** as follows:

Make a slipknot and keep the loop on the hook, insert the hook from front to back to front through the first marked st, yo and pull up a loop, yo and pull through 2 loops on the hook (first fpsc made). Work fpsc around the post of next 39 sts (1).

Fasten off and weave in the ends on WS.

FACE

Make 1 left and 1 right. Work in rows with a 9mm (M/N) hook and 3 strands of **MC**.

MUZZLE CHART

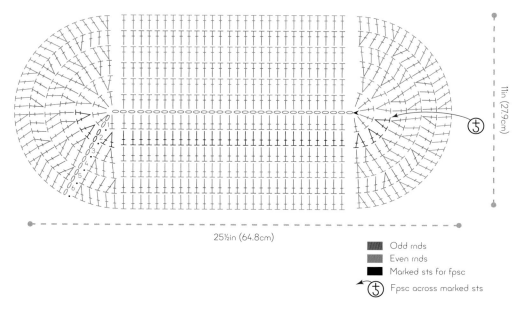

25½in (64.8cm)

11in (27.9cm)

- Odd rnds
- Even rnds
- Marked sts for fpsc
- (5) Fpsc across marked sts

LEFT AND RIGHT

To beg: Ch 6

Row 1: (RS) Dc in fourth ch from hook (3 skipped chs count as dc), dc in next ch, 6 dc in last ch, continue working across the bottom of the foundation ch, dc in next 3 chs; turn = 12 sts

Row 2: (WS) Ch 2 (counts as first dc now and throughout), skip first st, dc in next 2 sts, 2 dc in next 6 sts, dc in next 3 sts; turn = 18 sts

Row 3: (RS) Ch 2, skip first st, dc in next 2 sts, [2 dc in next st, dc in next st] 6 times, dc in next 3 sts = 24 sts

Fasten off, leaving a long single strand of **MC** for sewing. Weave in the other ends.

SMILEY EYES

Finish the left and right pieces in the same manner. With RS facing, skip 3 sts on each side of Row 2 and mark the middle 12 sts for the eye. Work around the marked stitches with a 9mm (M/N) hook and 3 strands of **CC1** as follows:

Make a slipknot and keep the loop on the hook, insert the hook from front to back to front through the first marked st, yo and pull up a loop, yo and pull through 2 loops on the hook (first fpsc made). Work fpsc around the post of next 11 sts (2).

Fasten off and weave in the ends on WS.

ASSEMBLING FACE

Place the left and the right pieces side by side with the flat edges facing down. Using the long **MC** tail between the pieces, whipstitch across 5 sts (3).

Fasten off and weave in the end. Keep the other long tail at the face edge for future assembling.

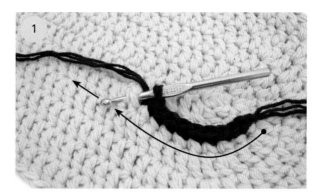

FACE CHART

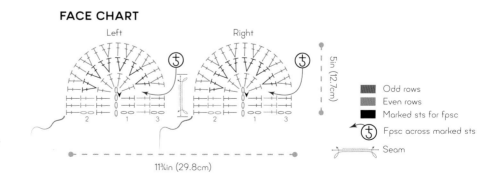

Left

Right

5in (12.7cm)

11¾in (29.8cm)

	Odd rows	
	Even rows	
	Marked sts for fpsc	
	Fpsc across marked sts	
	Seam	

HANDS

Make 2. Work in rows with a 9mm (M/N) hook and 3 strands of **MC**.

To beg: Ch 13

Row 1: (RS) 2 sc in second ch from hook (the skipped ch does not count as a st now and throughout), sc in next 10 chs, 2 sc in last ch; turn = 14 sts

Row 2: (WS) Ch 1 (does not count as a st now and throughout), 2 sc in first st, sc in next 13 sts; turn = 15 sts

Row 3: (RS) Ch 1, do not skip first st, sc2tog, sc in next 12 sts, 2 sc in last st; turn = 15 sts

Row 4: (WS) Ch 1, 2 sc in first st, sc in next 8 sts, ch 7; turn = 10 sts and 7 chs

Row 5: (RS) 2 sc in second ch from hook, sc in next 5 chs, sc in next 10 sts; turn = 17 sts

Row 6: (WS) Ch 1, sc in first st, sc in next 16 sts; turn = 17 sts

Row 7: (RS) Ch 1, do not skip first st, sc2tog, sc in next 15 sts; turn = 16 sts

Row 8: (WS) Ch 1, sc in first st, sc in next 9 sts, ch 7; turn = 10 sts and 7 chs

Rows 9-11: Repeat Rows 5-7

Row 12: (WS) Ch 1, do not skip first st, sc2tog, sc in next 8 sts, ch 7; turn = 9 sts and 7 chs

Row 13: (RS) 2 sc in second ch from hook, sc in next 5 chs, sc in next 7 sts, sc2tog; turn = 15 sts

Row 14: (WS) Ch 1, do not skip first st, sc2tog, sc in next 13 sts; turn = 14 sts

Row 15: (RS) Ch 1, do not skip first st, sc2tog, sc in next 10 sts, sc2tog = 12 sts

Fasten off and weave in the ends.

BANANA

Make 1. Work in rows with a 9mm (M/N) hook and 3 strands of yarn, changing colors (**CC3** and **CC2**) as indicated in the pattern.

To beg: With **CC3**, ch 5

Row 1: (WS) Sc in second ch from hook (the skipped ch does not count as a st), sc in next 3 chs; turn = 4 sts

Rows 2-5: Ch 1 (does not count as a st now and throughout), sc in first st, sc in next 3 sts; turn = 4 sts

Row 6: (RS) Ch 1, sc in first st, sc in next 3 sts, change to **CC2** and drop **CC3** (do not break off yarn); turn = 4 sts

Row 7: (WS) With **CC2**, ch 2 (counts as first dc now and throughout), dc in first st, dc in next 2 sts, 2 dc in last st; turn = 6 sts

Row 8: (RS) Ch 2, dc in first st, dc in next 4 sts, 2 dc in last st; turn = 8 sts

Row 9: (WS) Ch 2, dc in first st, dc in next 6 sts, 2 dc in last st; turn = 10 sts

Row 10: (RS) Ch 2, skip first st, dc in next 3 sts, hdc in next 3 sts, sc in next 3 sts; turn = 10 sts

Row 11: (WS) Ch 2, dc in first st, dc in next 8 sts, 2 dc in last st; turn = 12 sts

Row 12: (RS) Ch 2, skip first st, dc in next 3 sts, hdc in next 4 sts, sc in next 4 sts; turn = 12 sts

Row 13: (WS) Ch 2, dc in first st, dc in next 10 sts, 2 dc in last st; turn = 14 sts

Row 14: (RS) Ch 2, skip first st, dc in next 4 sts, hdc in next 5 sts, sc in next 4 sts; turn = 14 sts

Row 15: (WS) Ch 2, dc in first st, dc in next 12 sts, 2 dc in last st; turn = 16 sts

Row 16: (RS) Ch 2, skip first st, dc in next 5 sts, hdc in next 5 sts, sc in next 5 sts; turn = 16 sts

Row 17: (WS) Ch 2, dc in first st, dc in next 14 sts, 2 dc in last st; turn = 18 sts

HAND CHART

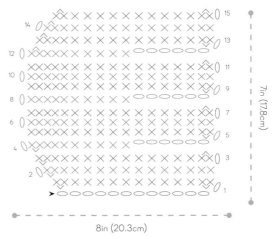

7in (17.8cm)

8in (20.3cm)

Row 18: (RS) Ch 2, skip first st, dc in next 5 sts, hdc in next 6 sts, sc in next 6 sts; turn = 18 sts

Row 19: (WS) Ch 2, skip first st, dc in next 17 sts; turn = 18 sts

Row 20: (RS) Ch 2, skip first st, dc in next 5 sts, hdc in next 6 sts, sc in next 6 sts; turn = 18 sts

Rows 21-46: Repeat Rows 19-20 in established pattern, ending on RS

Row 47: (WS) Ch 2, skip first st, dc2tog, dc in next 13 sts, dc2tog; turn = 16 sts

Row 48: (RS) Ch 2, skip first st, dc in next 5 sts, hdc in next 5 sts, sc in next 5 sts; turn = 16 sts

Row 49: (WS) Ch 2, skip first st, dc2tog, dc in next 11 sts, dc2tog; turn = 14 sts

Row 50: (RS) Ch 2, skip first st, dc in next 4 sts, hdc in next 5 sts, sc in next 4 sts; turn = 14 sts

Row 51: (WS) Ch 2, skip first st, dc2tog, dc in next 9 sts, dc2tog; turn = 12 sts

Row 52: (RS) Ch 2, skip first st, dc in next 3 sts, hdc in next 4 sts, sc in next 4 sts; turn = 12 sts

Row 53: (WS) Ch 2, skip first st, dc2tog, dc in next 7 sts, dc2tog; turn = 10 sts

Row 54: (RS) Ch 2, skip first st, dc in next 3 sts, hdc in next 3 sts, sc in next 3 sts; turn = 10 sts

Row 55: (WS) Ch 2, skip first st, dc2tog, dc in next 5 sts, dc2tog; turn = 8 sts

Row 56: (RS) Ch 2, skip first st, dc2tog, dc in next 3 sts, dc2tog; turn = 6 sts

Row 57: (WS) Ch 2, skip first st, dc2tog, dc in next st, dc2tog = 4 sts

Fasten off and weave in the ends.

EDGING

With RS facing, pick up **CC3** at the edge of Row 6 and work the edging as follows:

With **CC3**, ch 1 (does not count as a st), sc evenly around the edge of the stem, placing 3 sc in corners for increasing. Change to **CC2** and break off **CC3**, sc around the remaining edge of the banana, join (4). Fasten off and weave in the ends.

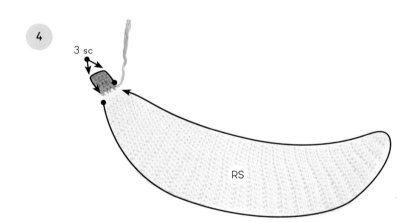

BANANA CHART

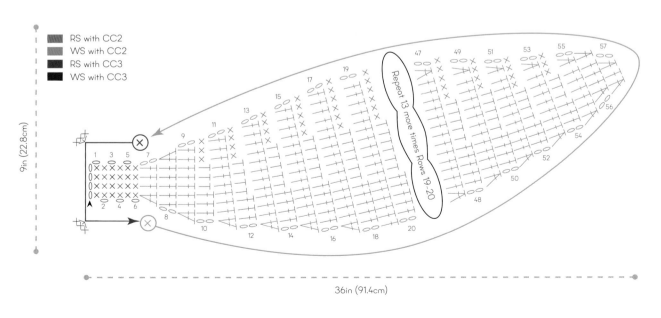

- RS with CC2
- WS with CC2
- RS with CC3
- WS with CC3

9in (22.8cm)

36in (91.4cm)

Repeat 13 more times Rows 19-20

ASSEMBLING RUG

With RS facing, assemble all pieces as follows (5):

Place the muzzle to cover the bottom edge of the head and backstitch across the overlapped edge with **MC**. Place the face right up against the muzzle, whipstitch across the bottom edge and backstitch around the remaining edge of the face with **MC**. Place the ears on each side of the head slightly above the muzzle and whipstitch across the edge with **CC1**. Place the banana to cover the bottom edge of the muzzle and backstitch across the overlapped edge with **CC2**.

Flip the rug to WS. Using the corresponding colors of yarn, whipstitch across the overlapped edges of the muzzle and the banana, whipstitch across the edges of the ears (6).

Finish the nose as follows:

Place the first marker 3 rounds below the joined center of the face, place the second and third markers 2 rows above the first marker in sixth stitch to the right and to the left (7).

Thread the needle with 2 strands of **CC3** and chain stitch the v-shaped nose from the right marker towards the next 2 markers (7), remove the markers.

Place the hands on each side of the banana, overlapping the fingers onto the banana.

Thread the needle with a single strand of **MC** and backstitch around the edge of the fingers (8).

If desired, make a removable non-slip lining (see General Techniques: Non-Slip Lining).

Make a bow using **CC4** to finish the monkey (see Common Shapes: Big Bow).

MONKEY PILLOW

SKILL LEVEL

FINISHED SIZE
17½in (44.5cm) diameter

HOOKS
3.75mm (F), 5.5mm (I)

YARN WEIGHT
4

NUMBER OF STRANDS
1

GAUGE WITH 1 STRAND AND 5.5MM (I) HOOK
14 sc x 16 rows = 4in x 4in (10cm x 10cm)

STITCH SUMMARY
Ch, sl st, sc, rsc, dc, picot, crest, arch, shell, join

SKILLS
Working in rows and in the round, working across the bottom of the foundation chain, changing colors, sewing

LEFT-HANDED CROCHET
Fully compatible

YARN

Abbreviation	Color	Amount
MC	Beige	93-109yd (85-100m)
CC1	Coffee	93-109yd (85-100m)
CC2	Yellow	Small amount
CC4	Lush Green	328-383yd (300-350m)
CC5	Red	Small amount

HEAD PILLOW BASE

BACK

Make 1. Work with a 5.5mm (I) hook and 1 strand of **CC4**. Follow the instructions for the round pillow (see Common Shapes: Round Pillow Base). Fasten off after finishing Rnd 25.

FRONT

Make 1. Work with a 5.5mm (I) hook and 1 strand of **CC1**. Follow the instructions for the round pillow base (see Common Shapes: Round Pillow Base). Change to **CC4** after Rnd 17, then continue working to Rnd 25 and do not break off yarn.

EDGING

Holding the front and the back pieces together with WS facing each other, work Rnd 26 through both pieces of fabric at the same time using the working yarn from the front piece.

Rnd 26: Ch 1 (does not count as a st now and throughout), sc in same st as previous sl st, sc in next 140 sts, stuff the pillow, sc in next 15 sts; join = 156 sts

Rnd 27: Ch 1, sc in same st as join, ch 5, skip st, [sc in next st, ch 5, skip st] 76 times, sc in next st, ch 2, skip st, dc in beg st (counts as last arch) = 78 arches

Rnd 28: Ch 1, sc in same sp, 9 dc in next arch, sc in next arch, [ch 5, sc in next arch, 9 dc in next arch, sc in next arch] 25 times, ch 2, dc in beg st (counts as last arch) = 26 shells and 26 arches

Rnd 29: Ch 1, sc in same sp, crest across next shell, [sc in next arch, crest across next shell] 25 times; join = 26 crests

Fasten off and weave in the ends.

MUZZLE

Make 1. Work in spiral rounds with a 5.5mm (I) hook and 1 strand of **MC**.

To beg: Ch 21

Rnd 1: Sc in second ch from hook (the skipped ch does not count as a st), sc in next 18 chs, 3 sc in last ch, continue working across the bottom of the foundation ch, sc in next 18 chs, 2 sc in last ch, do not join now and throughout = 42 sts

Rnd 2: 2 sc in first st of previous rnd, sc in next 18 sts, 2 sc in next 3 sts, sc in next 18 sts, 2 sc in next 2 sts = 48 sts

Rnd 3: Sc in next st, 2 sc in next st, sc in next 18 sts, [sc in next st, 2 sc in next st] 3 times, sc in next 18 sts, [sc in next st, 2 sc in next st] 2 times = 54 sts

Rnd 4: Sc in next 2 sts, 2 sc in next st, sc in next 18 sts, [sc in next 2 sts, 2 sc in next st] 3 times, sc in next 18 sts, [sc in next 2 sts, 2 sc in next st] 2 times = 60 sts

Rnd 5: Sc in next 3 sts, 2 sc in next st, sc in next 18 sts, [sc in next 3 sts, 2 sc in next st] 3 times, sc in next 18 sts, [sc in next 3 sts, 2 sc in next st] 2 times = 66 sts

Rnd 6: Sc in next 4 sts, 2 sc in next st, sc in next 18 sts, [sc in next 4 sts, 2 sc in next st] 3 times, sc in next 18 sts, [sc in next 4 sts, 2 sc in next st] 2 times = 72 sts

Rnd 7: Sc in next 5 sts, 2 sc in next st, sc in next 18 sts, [sc in next 5 sts, 2 sc in next st] 3 times, sc in next 18 sts, [sc in next 5 sts, 2 sc in next st] 2 times = 78 sts

Rnds 8-10: Sc in each st around = 78 sts

Sl st in next st and fasten off, leaving a long tail for sewing.

> **Use a stitch marker to mark the beginning of each round as you go.**

FACE

Make 1 left and 1 right. Work in rows with a 5.5mm (I) hook and 1 strand of **MC**.

LEFT AND RIGHT

To beg: Ch 6

Row 1: (RS) Sc in second ch from hook (the skipped ch does not count as a st), sc in next 3 chs, 3 sc in last ch, continue working across the bottom of the foundation ch, sc in next 4 chs; turn = 11 sts

Row 2: (WS) Ch 1 (does not count as a st now and throughout), sc in first st, sc in next 3 sts, 2 sc in next 3 sts, sc in next 4 sts; turn = 14 sts

Row 3: (RS) Ch 1, sc in first st, sc in next 3 sts, [2 sc in next st, sc in next st] 3 times, sc in next 4 sts; turn = 17 sts

Row 4: (WS) Ch 1, sc in first st, sc in next 3 sts, [2 sc in next st, sc in next 2 sts] 3 times, sc in next 4 sts; turn = 20 sts

Row 5: (RS) Ch 1, sc in first st, sc in next 3 sts, [2 sc in next st, sc in next 3 sts] 3 times, sc in next 4 sts; turn = 23 sts

Fasten off, leaving a long tail for sewing. Weave in the end from the beg.

1

ASSEMBLING FACE

Place the left and the right pieces side by side with the flat edges facing down. Using the long **MC** tail between the pieces, whipstitch across 6 sts (1), fasten off and weave in the end. Keep the other long tail at the face edge for future assembly.

EARS

Make 2. Work in rows with a 5.5mm (I) hook and 1 strand of yarn, changing colors (**MC** and **CC1**) as indicated in the pattern.

To beg: With **MC**, ch 2

Row 1: (RS) 3 sc in second ch from hook (the skipped ch does not count as a st); turn = 3 sts

Row 2: (WS) Ch 1 (does not count as a st now and throughout), 2 sc in first st, 2 sc in next 2 sts; turn = 6 sts

Row 3: (RS) Ch 1, 2 sc in first st, sc in next st, [2 sc in next st, sc in next st] 2 times; turn = 9 sts

Row 4: (WS) Ch 1, 2 sc in first st, sc in next 2 sts, [2 sc in next st, sc in next 2 sts] 2 times, change to **CC1** and break off **MC**; turn = 12 sts

Row 5: (RS) With **CC1**, ch 1, 2 sc in first st, sc in next 3 sts, [2 sc in next st, sc in next 3 sts] 2 times; do not turn = 15 sts

Row 6: (RS) Ch 1, skip first st, rsc in next 13 sts, sl st in next st = 14 sts

Fasten off, leaving a long tail for sewing. Weave in the other ends.

PILLOW BASE EDGING CHART

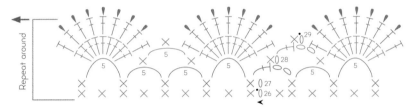

FACE CHART

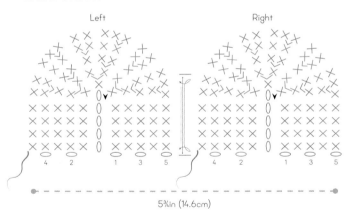

Left   Right

5¾in (14.6cm)

EAR CHART

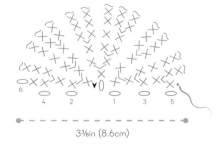

3⅜in (8.6cm)

ASSEMBLING PILLOW

Place the muzzle approximately 6 rounds below the center of the head, covering the color change between Rnds 17 and 18. Using the long **MC** tail, whipstitch around the muzzle, leaving an opening at the end for stuffing. Stuff the muzzle and complete sewing (2).

Place the face above the muzzle with its straight edge right up against the muzzle. Using the long **MC** tail, whipstitch across the bottom edge and backstitch around the remaining edge of the face (3).

Using a single strand of **CC1**, chain stitch the eyes 2 rows below the face edge and chain stitch the v-shaped nose (4).

Using a single strand of **CC5**, chain stitch the smile (5).

Place the ears on each side of the head slightly above the muzzle. Whipstitch each ear across the straight edge on RS and WS using the long **CC1** tail (6 and 7).

Cut 6 strands of **CC1** approximately 9in (23cm) long and fold the bundle in half. Using a crochet hook, pull the bundle through the stitches on the top of the head to create a loop (8), pull the loose ends through the loop and tighten up the tassel. Trim the ends to desired length.

If desired, make a small bow using 1 strand of **CC2** (see Common Shapes: Small Bow). Place the bow onto the head and backstitch around the center using the long tail from the bow (9).

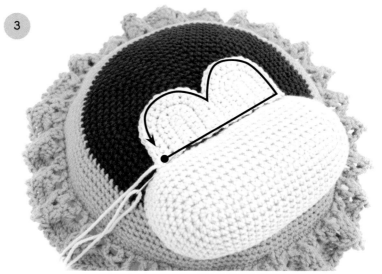

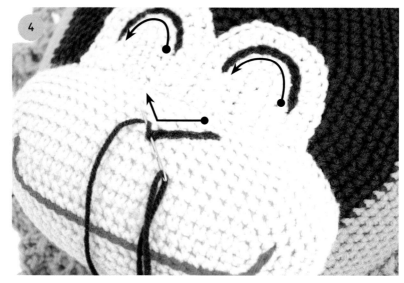

A small bow tie will make your monkey even cuter (10)!

MONKEY TOY BAG

SKILL LEVEL

FINISHED SIZE
18½in x 30½in (47cm x 77.5cm)

HOOKS
3.75mm (F), 5.5mm (I), 9mm (M/N)

YARN WEIGHT
4

NUMBER OF STRANDS
1, 2 and 3

**GAUGE WITH 2 STRANDS
AND 9MM (M/N) HOOK**
10 dc x 5 rows = 4in x 4in (10cm x 10cm)

STITCH SUMMARY
Ch, sl st, sc, sc2tog, rsc, hdc, dc,
picot, crest, arch, shell, join

SKILLS
Working in rows and in the
round, working across the
bottom of the foundation chain,
changing colors, sewing

LEFT-HANDED CROCHET
Fully compatible

YARN

Abbreviation	Color	Amount
CC4	Lush Green	601-656yd (550-600m)
CC6	Carrot	546-601yd (500-550m)

All other colors and amounts are the
same as for the Monkey Pillow.

TOY BAG

Make 1. Work in the round with a 9mm (M/N) hook and 2 strands of yarn, changing colors (**CC6** and **CC4**) in every round until 3 rounds remain. Begin with **CC6**.

To beg: Ch 3, sl st in third ch from hook to form a ring (or start with a magic ring)

Rnd 1: Ch 2 (does not count as a st now and throughout), 12 dc in ring; join = 12 sts

Rnd 2: Ch 2, 2 dc in same st as join, 2 dc in next 11 sts; join = 24 sts

Rnd 3: Ch 2, dc in same st as join, 2 dc in next st, [dc in next st, 2 dc in next st] 11 times; join = 36 sts

Rnd 4: Ch 2, dc in same st as join, dc in next st, 2 dc in next st, [dc in next 2 sts, 2 dc in next st] 11 times; join = 48 sts

Rnd 5: Ch 2, dc in same st as join, dc in next 2 sts, 2 dc in next st, [dc in next 3 sts, 2 dc in next st] 11 times; join = 60 sts

Rnd 6: Ch 2, dc in same st as join, dc in next 3 sts, 2 dc in next st, [dc in next 4 sts, 2 dc in next st] 11 times; join = 72 sts

Rnd 7: Ch 2, dc in same st as join, dc in next 4 sts, 2 dc in next st, [dc in next 5 sts, 2 dc in next st] 11 times; join = 84 sts

Rnd 8: Ch 2, dc in same st as join, dc in next 12 sts, 2 dc in next st, [dc in next 13 sts, 2 dc in next st] 5 times; join = 90 sts

Rnds 9-35: Ch 2, dc in same st as join, dc in next 89 sts; join = 90 sts

Break off **CC6** and continue to work the remaining rounds with **CC4**:

Rnd 36: Ch 1, sc in same st as join, ch 5, skip 2 sts, [sc in next st, ch 5, skip 2 sts] 28 times, sc in next st, ch 2, skip 2 sts, dc in beg st (counts as last arch) = 30 arches

Rnd 37: Ch 1, sc in same sp, 9 dc in next arch, sc in next arch, [ch 5, sc in next arch, 9 dc in next arch, sc in next arch] 9 times, ch 2, dc in beg st (counts as last arch) = 10 shells and 10 arches

Rnd 38: Ch 1, sc in same sp, crest across next shell, [sc in next arch, crest across next shell] 9 times; join = 10 crests

Fasten off and weave in the ends.

DRAWSTRING

Make 1. Work with a 9mm (M/N) hook and 3 strands of **CC1**.

To beg: Ch 140

Fasten off and trim the ends.

BANANAS

Make 2. Work in the round with a 3.75mm (F) hook and 1 strand of yarn, changing colors (**CC1** and **CC2**) as indicated in the pattern.

To beg: With **CC1**, ch 3, sl st in third ch from hook to form a ring (or start with a magic ring)

Rnd 1: Ch 1 (does not count as a st now and throughout), 6 sc in ring; join = 6 sts

Rnd 2: Ch 1, sc in same st as join, 2 sc in next st, [sc in next st, 2 sc in next st] 2 times, change to **CC2** and break off **CC1**; join = 9 sts

Rnd 3: With **CC2**, ch 1, sc in same st as join, sc in next st, hdc in next 6 sts, sc in next st; join = 9 sts

Rnd 4: Ch 1, sc in same st as join, sc in next st, 2 hdc in next st, hdc in next 4 sts, 2 hdc in next st, 2 sc in next st; join = 12 sts

Rnds 5-12: Ch 1, sc in same st as join, sc in next st, hdc in next 8 sts, sc in next 2 sts; join = 12 sts

Rnd 13: Ch 1, sc in same st as join, sc in next st, sc2tog, [sc in next 2 sts, sc2tog] 2 times; join = 9 sts

Rnd 14: Ch 1, sc in same st as join, sc in next 8 sts; join and stuff the banana = 9 sts

Rnd 15: Ch 1, sc in same st as join, [sc2tog] 4 times; join = 5 sts

Fasten off, leaving a long tail for sewing.

Use up yarn scraps by changing colors in every round of the bag.

BANANA CUPS

Make 2. Work in spiral rounds with a 3.75mm (F) hook and 1 strand of **CC4**.

To beg: Ch 5, sl st in fifth ch from hook to form a ring

Rnd 1: Ch 1 (does not count as a st), 10 sc in ring; do not join now and throughout = 10 sts

Rnds 2-4: Sc in first st of previous rnd, sc in next 9 sts = 10 sts

Sl st in next st, fasten off and weave in the ends.

MONKEY HEAD

Make 1. Work with a 5.5mm (I) hook and 1 strand of **CC1**. Follow the head instructions of the Monkey Rug from the beginning to Row 6 (see Monkey Rug: Head). Continue to work edging as follows:

Edge: (RS) Ch 1 (does not count as a st), sc in first st, sc in next 21 sts, [ch 10, sc in next st] 3 times, sc in next 21 sts = 46 sts and 3 ch-10 loops

Fasten off, leaving a long tail for sewing.

MONKEY MUZZLE, FACE AND EARS

Follow the instructions for the muzzle, face and ears from the Monkey Pillow (see Monkey Pillow: Muzzle, Monkey Pillow: Face and Monkey Pillow: Ears).

Make a bow using **CC2** (see Common Shapes: Small Bow).

ASSEMBLING TOY BAG

Position the head and the muzzle in the middle of the bag. Backstitch around the head edge using the long **CC1** tail. Using the long **MC** tail, whipstitch around the muzzle, leaving an opening at the end for stuffing. Stuff the muzzle and complete sewing (1).

Place the face above the muzzle with its straight edge right up against the muzzle. Using the long **MC** tail,

whipstitch across the bottom edge and backstitch around the remaining edge of the face (2).

Place the ears on each side of the head slightly above the muzzle. Using the long **CC1** tail, whipstitch each ear across the straight edge and backstitch around the remaining edge (2).

Chain stitch the eyes, nose and smile (3), following the instructions for the Monkey Pillow (see Monkey Pillow: Assembling Pillow).

If desired, make a small bow (see Common Shapes: Small Bow) using 1 strand of **CC2**. Place the bow onto the head and backstitch around the center (4).

Using a crochet hook, thread the drawstring through the arches of the bag under the shells (5).

Insert the ends of the drawstrings through the cups into banana openings. Using the long **CC2** tail, whipstitch around each banana opening to secure. Slide the cups down to cover the seams (6).

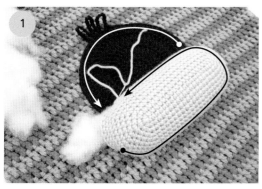

CRANKY THE CRAB

Rug, Pillow and Security Blanket

Like some children, crabs are independent and feisty. They like to do their own things and often get a bad reputation for being cranky. They just have their minds made up on what they want to do and don't like being interrupted.

When you think of the ocean and sandy beaches, I bet you think of our crusty friends, crabs. Most children find them fun and interesting, even though they are the best pinchers! Do not worry, Cranky the Crab has pincers made from yarn so they are soft and safe for kids to interact with. This adorable crab collection will lighten up your home or cottage with a fresh and crisp marine habitat.

CRAB RUG

SKILL LEVEL

FINISHED SIZE
42in x 30½in (106.7cm x 77.5cm)

HOOKS
3.75mm (F), 5mm (H),
5.5mm (I), 9mm (M/N)

YARN WEIGHT
4

NUMBER OF STRANDS
1 and 3

**GAUGE WITH 3 STRANDS
AND 9MM (M/N) HOOK**
9 dc x 4.5 rows = 4in x 4in (10cm x 10cm)

STITCH SUMMARY
Ch, sl st, sc, sc2tog, dc, join

SKILLS
Working in rows and in the round,
raw edge finishing, working across
the bottom of the foundation chain,
changing colors, blocking, sewing

LEFT-HANDED CROCHET
See Crochet Techniques:
Left-Handed Crochet

YARN

Abbreviation	Color	Amount
MC	Flamingo or Coral	1093-1421yd (1000-1300m)
CC1	Black	109-131yd (100-120m)
CC2	White	Small amount
CC3	Aquamarine	Small amount

BODY CHART

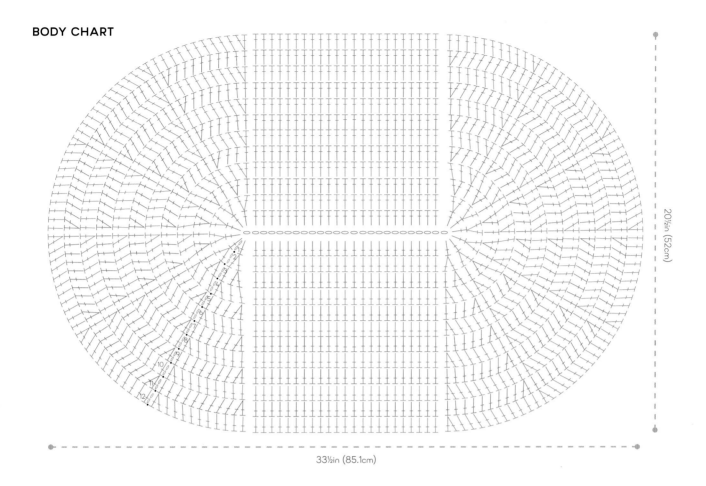

20½in (52cm)

33½in (85.1cm)

BODY

Make 1. Work in the round with a 9mm (M/N) hook and 3 strands of **MC**.

To beg: Ch 27

Rnd 1: Dc in third ch from hook (2 skipped chs do not count as a st), dc in next 23 chs, 6 dc in last ch, continue working across the bottom of the foundation ch, dc in next 23 chs, 5 dc in last ch; join = 58 sts

Rnd 2: Ch 2 (does not count as a st now and throughout), 2 dc in same st as join, dc in next 23 sts, 2 dc in next 6 sts, dc in next 23 sts, 2 dc in next 5 sts; join = 70 sts

Rnd 3: Ch 2, dc in same st as join, 2 dc in next st, dc in next 23 sts, [dc in next st, 2 dc in next st] 6 times, dc in next 23 sts, [dc in next st, 2 dc in next st] 5 times; join = 82 sts

Rnd 4: Ch 2, 2 dc in same st as join, dc in next 25 sts, [2 dc in next st, dc in next 2 sts] 6 times, dc in next 23 sts, [2 dc in next st, dc in next 2 sts] 5 times; join = 94 sts

Rnd 5: Ch 2, dc in same st as join, dc in next 2 sts, 2 dc in next st, dc in next 23 sts, [dc in next 3 sts, 2 dc in next st] 6 times, dc in next 23 sts, [dc in next 3 sts, 2 dc in next st] 5 times; join = 106 sts

Rnd 6: Ch 2, 2 dc in same st as join, dc in next 27 sts, [2 dc in next st, dc in next 4 sts] 6 times, dc in next 23 sts, [2 dc in next st, dc in next 4 sts] 5 times; join = 118 sts

Rnd 7: Ch 2, dc in same st as join, dc in next 4 sts, 2 dc in next st, dc in next 23 sts, [dc in next 5 sts, 2 dc in next st] 6 times, dc in next 23 sts, [dc in next 5 sts, 2 dc in next st] 5 times; join = 130 sts

Rnd 8: Ch 2, 2 dc in same st as join, dc in next 29 sts, [2 dc in next st, dc in next 6 sts] 6 times, dc in next 23 sts, [2 dc in next st, dc in next 6 sts] 5 times; join = 142 sts

Rnd 9: Ch 2, dc in same st as join, dc in next 6 sts, 2 dc in next st, dc in next 23 sts, [dc in next 7 sts, 2 dc in next st] 6 times, dc in next 23 sts, [dc in next 7 sts, 2 dc in next st] 5 times; join = 154 sts

Rnd 10: Ch 2, 2 dc in same st as join, dc in next 31 sts, [2 dc in next st, dc in next 8 sts] 6 times, dc in next 23 sts, [2 dc in next st, dc in next 8 sts] 5 times; join = 166 sts

Rnd 11: Ch 2, dc in same st as join, dc in next 8 sts, 2 dc in next st, dc in next 23 sts, [dc in next 9 sts, 2 dc in next st] 6 times, dc in next 23 sts, [dc in next 9 sts, 2 dc in next st] 5 times; join = 178 sts

Rnd 12: Ch 2, 2 dc in same st as join, dc in next 33 sts, [2 dc in next st, dc in next 10 sts] 6 times, dc in next 23 sts, [2 dc in next st, dc in next 10 sts] 5 times; join = 190 sts

Fasten off and weave in the ends.

Use stitch markers to indicate the start of spiral rounds.

EYES

BASIC EYES

Make 2. Follow the instructions for the basic eyes (see Common Shapes: Basic Eyes). Use 1 strand of **CC1** with a 5mm (H) hook for the pupils and 1 strand of **CC2** with a 3.75mm (F) hook for the highlights.

IRISES

Make 2. Work in spiral rounds with a 5mm (H) hook and 1 strand of **CC3**.

To beg: Ch 3, sl st in third ch from hook to form a ring (or start with a magic ring)

Rnd 1: Ch 1 (does not count as a st), 6 sc in ring; do not join now and throughout = 6 sts

Rnd 2: 2 sc in first st of previous rnd, 2 sc in next 5 sts = 12 sts

Rnd 3: 2 sc in each st around = 24 sts

Rnd 4: Sc in each st around = 24 sts

Sl st in next st, fasten off, leaving a long tail for sewing.

ASSEMBLING EYES

Place the basic eyes on top of the irises and backstitch around using **CC1**.

EYELIDS

Make 2. Work in rows from the top down, using a 5.5mm (I) hook and 1 strand of **MC**.

To beg: Ch 8

Row 1: (RS) 2 sc in second ch from hook (the skipped ch does not count as a st), sc in next 5 chs, 2 sc in last ch; turn = 9 sts

Row 2: (WS) Ch 1 (does not count as a st now and throughout), 2 sc in first st, sc in next 7 sts, 2 sc in last st; turn = 11 sts

Row 3: (RS) Ch 1, 2 sc in first st, sc in next 9 sts, 2 sc in last st; turn = 13 sts

Row 4: (WS) Ch 1, 2 sc in first st, sc in next 11 sts, 2 sc in last st; turn = 15 sts

Row 5: (RS) Ch 1, 2 sc in first st, sc in next 13 sts, 2 sc in last st; do not turn = 17 sts

Rotate the work in a clockwise direction (or in a counter-clockwise direction for left-handed crochet) and continue to work edging as follows:

Edge: (RS) Ch 1, sc evenly across the raw edges towards the beg of Row 5

Fasten off, leaving a long tail for sewing.

EYESTALKS

Make 2. Work in the round with a 9mm (M/N) hook and 3 strands of yarn, changing colors (**CC2** and **MC**) as indicated in the pattern.

To beg: With **CC2**, ch 3, sl st in third ch from hook to form a ring (or start with a magic ring)

Rnd 1: Ch 1 (does not count as a st now and throughout), 6 sc in ring; join = 6 sts

Rnd 2: Ch 1, 2 sc in same st as join, 2 sc in next 5 sts; join = 12 sts

Rnd 3: Ch 1, 2 sc in same st as join, 2 sc in next 11 sts, change to **MC** and break off **CC2**; join = 24 sts

Rnd 4: With **MC**, ch 1, sc in same st as join, sc in next 20 sts, ch 6, sc in second ch from hook, sc in next 4 chs, sc in next 2 sts of circle; turn, (WS) skip 2 sc just made, sc in next 5 sts; turn, (RS) ch 1, sc in first st, sc in next 4 sts, sc in last st of circle; join = 24 sts around circle and 3 rows of sideways sts

Fasten off and weave in the ends.

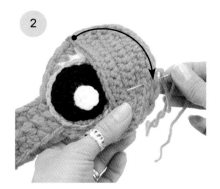

ASSEMBLING EYESTALKS

Position the eye along the bottom **CC2** edge of the eyestalk and backstitch around using **CC3** (1).

Place the curved edge of the eyelid along the top edge of the eyestalk, covering part of the eye. Whipstitch around the curved edge using **MC** (2). Finish the second eyestalk in the same manner.

LEGS

Make 6. Work in rows with a 9mm (M/N) hook and 3 strands of **MC**.

To beg: Ch 11

Row 1: (WS) Sc in second ch from hook (the skipped ch does not count as a st), sc in next 8 chs, 3 sc in last ch, continue working across the bottom of the foundation ch, sc in next 9 chs; turn = 21 sts

Row 2: (RS) Ch 1 (does not count as a st), sc in first st, sc in next 8 sts, 2 sc in next 3 sts, sc in next 9 sts = 24 sts

Fasten off, leaving a long single strand of **MC** for sewing. Weave in the other ends.

IRIS CHART

2½in (6.3cm)

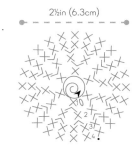

EYESTALK CHART

4¼in (10.8cm)

6¼in (15.9cm)

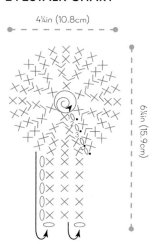

EYELID CHART

4¼in (10.8cm)

2in (5.1cm)

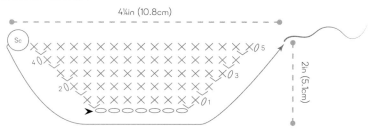

LEG CHART

4¾in (12cm)

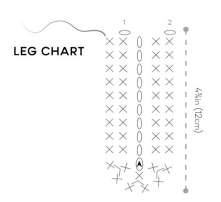

PINCERS

Make 1 left and 1 right pincer. Work in rows with a 9mm (M/N) hook and 3 strands of **MC**.

LEFT PINCER

To beg: Ch 12

Row 1: (RS) 2 dc in fourth ch from hook (3 skipped chs count as first dc), dc in next 7 chs, 6 dc in last ch, continue working across the bottom of the foundation ch, dc in next 7 chs, 3 dc in last ch; turn = 26 sts

Row 2: (WS) Ch 3 (counts as first dc now and throughout), 2 dc in first st, dc in next 9 sts, 2 dc in next 6 sts, dc in next 9 sts, 3 dc in last st; turn = 36 sts

Row 3: (RS) Ch 3, 2 dc in first st, dc in next 11 sts, [2 dc in next st, dc in next st] 6 times, dc in next 11 sts, 3 dc in last st; turn = 46 sts

Row 4: (WS) Ch 3, 2 dc in first st, dc in next 13 sts, [2 dc in next st, dc in next 2 sts] 6 times, dc in next 13 sts, 3 dc in last st; turn = 56 sts

Row 5: (RS) Ch 1 (does not count as a st), sc in first st, sc in next 26 sts; work arm – ch 21, sc in second ch from hook, sc in next 19 chs, sc in next 2 sts of pincer; turn, (WS) skip 2 sc just made, [sc in next 2 sts of arm, sc2tog] 5 times; turn, (RS) ch 1, do not skip st, [sc2tog, sc in next st of arm] 5 times, sc in next st of pincer; continue to work across pincer, sc in next 26 sts; do not turn = 56 sts of pincer and 3 rows of arm

To finish, rotate the work in a clockwise direction (or in a counter-clockwise direction for left-handed crochet), ch 1, sc evenly across the raw edges towards the beg of Row 5.

Fasten off and weave in the ends. Spray block if necessary (see General Techniques: Blocking).

RIGHT PINCER

Work from the beginning to Row 4, same as for left pincer. Continue the next row as follows:

Row 5: (RS) Ch 1 (does not count as a st), sc in first st, sc in next 26 sts; work arm – ch 11 loosely, 2 sc in second ch from hook, sc in next ch, [2 sc in next ch, sc in next ch] 4 times, sc in next 2 sts of pincer; turn, (WS) skip 2 sc just made, [sc in next 2 sts of arm, 2 sc in next st] 5 times; turn, (RS) ch 1, sc in first st, sc in next 19 sts of arm, sc in next st of pincer; continue to work across pincer, sc in next 26 sts; do not turn = 56 sts of pincer and 3 rows of arm

Finish as for left pincer.

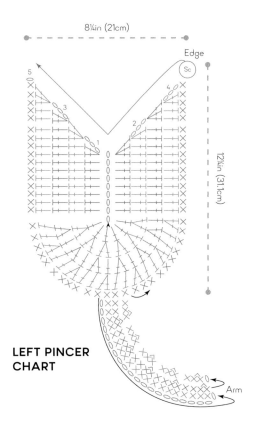

LEFT PINCER CHART

8¼in (21cm)

12¼in (31.1cm)

Edge

Sc

Arm

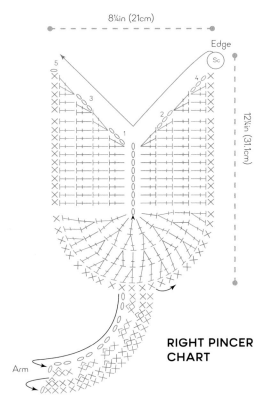

RIGHT PINCER CHART

8¼in (21cm)

12¼in (31.1cm)

Edge

Sc

Arm

BOW (OPTIONAL)

Make 1. Follow the instructions for the big bow using **CC1** (see Common Shapes: Big Bow).

ASSEMBLING RUG

Place the eyestalks tight up against the top edge of the body, leaving a space of 29 stitches in the middle between the eyestalks (3). Whipstitch across RS using **MC**, do not break off yarn.

Place 3 legs on each side of the body, leaving a space of 47 stitches in the middle of the bottom edge and a space of 2 stitches between the legs in each group (3). Whipstitch across RS using **MC**, do not break off yarn.

Place the pincers on each side of the body between the legs and the eyestalks (3).

Whipstitch the pincers across the corresponding edges of the body and the eyestalks using **MC** (4), do not break off yarn.

Flip the rug to WS and whipstitch across the same edges using **MC** tails from each piece (5).

Thread the needle with 2 strands of **CC1** and chain stitch a crooked smile approximately between the fourth and the sixth rounds below the body edge (6).

If using, position the bow below the crooked smile and backstitch around the center with a single strand of **CC1** (6). Keep the side edges of the bow unattached or whipstitch the corners to keep them in place.

If desired, make a removable non-slip lining (see General Techniques: Non-Slip Lining).

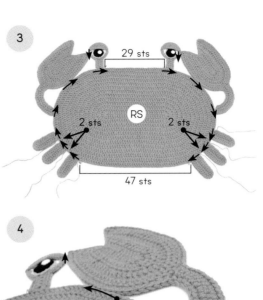

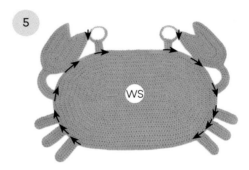

CRAB PILLOW

SKILL LEVEL

  ○ ○

FINISHED SIZE
26in x 20in (66cm x 50.8cm)

HOOKS
3.75mm (F), 4.25mm (G),
5mm (H), 5.5mm (I), 6mm (J)

YARN WEIGHT
4

NUMBER OF STRANDS
1 and 2

**GAUGE WITH 1 STRAND
AND 5.5MM (I) HOOK**
14 sc x 16 rows = 4in x 4in (10cm x 10cm)

STITCH SUMMARY
Ch, sl st, sc, sc2tog, hdc, dc, join

SKILLS
Working in rows and in the round,
raw edge finishing, working across
the bottom of the foundation
chain, changing colors, sewing

LEFT-HANDED CROCHET
See Crochet Techniques:
Left-Handed Crochet

YARN

Abbreviation	Color	Amount
MC	Flamingo or Coral	874-929yd (800-850m)
CC4	Green (optional)	Small amount

All other contrasting colors are the same as
for the Crab Rug (small amount of each).

PILLOW BASE

Make 1 front and 1 back using 1 strand of **MC** with a 5.5mm (I) hook. Follow the instructions for the oval pillow base (see Common Shapes: Oval Pillow Base). Fasten off after finishing the back piece, but do not break off yarn after finishing the front piece.

Holding the front and the back pieces together with WS facing each other, work the joining round through both pieces of fabric at the same time, using the working yarn from the front piece.

Rnd 26: Ch 1 (does not count as a st), sc in same st as previous sl st, sc in next 180 sts, stuff the pillow, sc in next 15 sts; join = 196 sts

Fasten off and weave in the ends.

EYES

BASIC EYES

Make 2. Follow the instructions for the basic eyes (see Common Shapes: Basic Eyes). Work with a 4.25mm (G) hook and 1 strand of **CC1** for the pupils and 1 strand of **CC2** for the highlights.

IRISES

Make 2. Work in the round with a 5mm (H) hook and 1 strand of **CC3**.

To beg: Ch 3, sl st in third ch from hook to form a ring (or start with a magic ring)

Rnd 1: Ch 1 (does not count as a st now and throughout), 8 hdc in ring; join = 8 sts

Rnd 2: Ch 1, 2 hdc in same st as join, 2 hdc in next 7 sts; join = 16 sts

Rnd 3: Ch 1, sc in same st as join, sc in next 2 sts, 2 sc in next st, [sc in next 3 sts, 2 sc in next st] 3 times; join = 20 sts

Fasten off, leaving a long tail for sewing.

OUTER EYES

Make 2. Follow the instructions for the irises in the Crab Rug (see Crab Rug: Eyes), using a 5.5mm (I) hook and 1 strand of **CC2**.

ASSEMBLING EYES

Place the basic eyes on top of the irises and backstitch around using **CC1**. Place the irises on top of the outer eyes and backstitch around using **CC3**.

EYELIDS

Make 2. Work in spiral rounds with a 5.5mm (I) hook and 1 strand of **MC**.

To beg: Ch 3, sl st in third ch from hook to form a ring (or start with a magic ring)

Rnd 1: Ch 1 (does not count as a st), 6 sc in ring, do not join now and throughout = 6 sts

Rnd 2: 2 sc in first st of previous rnd, 2 sc in next 5 sts = 12 sts

Rnd 3: [Sc in next st, 2 sc in next st] 6 times = 18 sts

Rnd 4: [Sc in next 2 sts, 2 sc in next st] 6 times = 24 sts

Rnd 5: [Sc in next 3 sts, 2 sc in next st] 6 times = 30 sts

Rnd 6: [Sc in next 4 sts, 2 sc in next st] 6 times = 36 sts

Rnds 7-10: Sc in each st around = 36 sts

Sl st in next st, fasten off, leaving a long tail for sewing.

EYESTALKS

Make 2. Work in spiral rounds with a 5.5mm (I) hook and 1 strand of **MC**. Stuff as you go.

To beg: Ch 3, sl st in third ch from hook to form a ring (or start with a magic ring)

Rnds 1-5: Same as Rnds 1-5 of eyelids

Rnds 6-10: Sc in each st around = 30 sts

Rnd 11: [Sc in next 3 sts, sc2tog] = 24 sts

Rnd 12: [Sc in next 2 sts, sc2tog] = 18 sts

Rnd 13: [Sc in next st, sc2tog] = 12 sts

Rnds 14-19: Sc in each st around = 12 sts

Sl st in next st, fasten off, leaving a long tail for sewing.

Use stitch markers to indicate the start of spiral rounds.

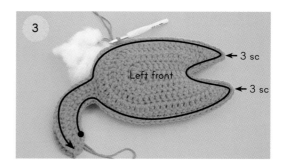

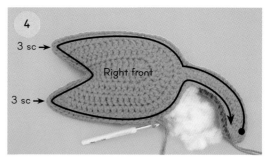

ASSEMBLING EYESTALKS

Position the eyes on the eyestalks and backstitch around using **CC2** (1).

Position the eyelids on top of the eyestalks, partially covering the eyes and backstitch around using **MC** (2).

PINCERS

Make 2. Work in rows with a 6mm (J) hook and 2 strands of **MC**.

FRONT AND BACK

Make 2 pieces following the left pincer instructions in the Crab Rug from the beginning to Row 5 (see Crab Rug: Left Pincer).

Fasten off and weave in the ends. Label the first piece as "Left front" and label the second piece as "Right back".

Make 2 pieces following the right pincer instructions in the Crab Rug from the beginning to Row 5 (see Crab Rug: Right Pincer).

Fasten off and weave in the ends. Label the first piece as "Left back" and label the second piece as "Right front".

ASSEMBLING LEFT PINCER

Place the left-front piece on top of the left-back piece with WS together. Join yarn at the bottom edge of the arm and work sc around the edge through the stitches of both pieces to join them, placing 3 sc in corners for increasing. Stuff lightly as you go (3).

Do not join the end opening of the arm. Fasten off, leaving a long single strand of **MC** for sewing, hide all the other ends inside of the arm.

ASSEMBLING RIGHT PINCER

Place the right-front piece on top of the right-back piece with WS together. Join yarn at the bottom edge of the arm and work sc around the edge through the stitches of both pieces to join them, placing 3 sc in corners for increasing. Stuff lightly as you go (4).

Do not join the end opening of the arm. Fasten off, leaving a long single strand of **MC** for sewing, hide all the other ends inside of the arm.

LEGS

Make 6. Work in spiral rounds with a 5.5mm (I) hook and 1 strand of **MC**. Stuff as you go.

To beg: Ch 3, sl st in third ch from hook to form a ring (or start with a magic ring)

Rnd 1: Ch 1 (does not count as a st), 6 sc in ring; do not join now and throughout = 6 sts

Rnd 2: 2 sc in first st of previous rnd, 2 sc in next 5 sts = 12 sts

Rnd 3: [Sc in next st, 2 sc in next st] 6 times = 18 sts

Rnds 4-13: Sc in each st around = 18 sts

Sl st in next st, fasten off, leaving a long tail for sewing.

BOW (OPTIONAL)

Make 1. Follow the instructions for the small bow using **CC4** (see Common Shapes: Small Bow).

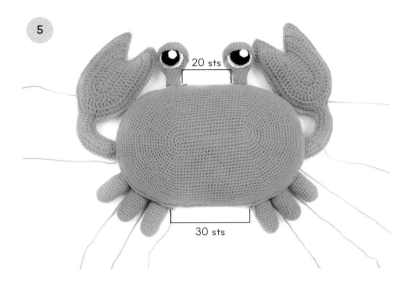

5

20 sts

30 sts

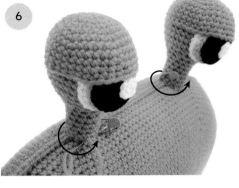

6

7

8

9

ASSEMBLING PILLOW

Place the eyestalks tight up against the top edge of the body (pillow base), leaving a space of 20 stitches in the middle between the eyestalks (5). Whipstitch twice around using **MC** (6).

Place 3 legs on each side of the body (pillow base), leaving a space of 30 stitches in the middle of the bottom edge and no spaces between the legs in each group (5). Whipstitch twice around using **MC** (7).

Place the pincers on each side of the body (pillow base) between the legs and the eyestalks (5). Whipstitch the pincers twice around the corresponding edges of the body and the eyestalks using **MC** (8).

Thread the needle with a single strand of **CC1** and chain stitch a crooked smile below the right eye (9).

If using, position the bow below the crooked smile and backstitch around the center using **CC4** (9).

CRAB SECURITY BLANKET

SKILL LEVEL

FINISHED SIZE
19½in x 19½in (49.5cm x 49.5cm)

HOOKS
3.75mm (F), 5mm (H), 6mm (J)

YARN WEIGHT
4

NUMBER OF STRANDS
1 and 2

**GAUGE WITH 1 STRAND
AND 5MM (H) HOOK**
15 dc x 8 rows = 4in x 4in (10cm x 10cm)

STITCH SUMMARY
Ch, sl st, sc, sc2tog, hdc,
dc, tr, picot, join

SKILLS
Working in rows and in the round,
raw edge finishing, changing
colors, blocking, sewing

LEFT-HANDED CROCHET
Fully compatible

YARN

Abbreviation	Color	Amount
CC3	Aquamarine	240-273yd (220-250m)
CC4	Variegated Blue	207-240yd (190-220m)

All other colors are the same as for the
Crab Rug (small amount of each).

BLANKET

Make 1. Work in rows with a 5mm (H) hook and 1 strand of yarn, changing colors (**CC3** and **CC4**) as indicated in the pattern.

To beg: With **CC4**, ch 71

Row 1: (WS) Sc in second ch from hook (the skipped ch does not count as a st), sc in next 69 chs; change to **CC3** and turn = 70 sts

Row 2: (RS) With **CC3**, ch 1 (does not count as a st now and throughout), sc in first st, hdc in next st, dc in next 2 sts, tr in next 2 sts, dc in next 2 sts, hdc in next 2 sts, [sc in next 2 sts, hdc in next 2 sts, dc in next 2 sts, tr in next 2 sts, dc in next 2 sts, hdc in next 2 sts] 4 times, sc in next 2 sts, hdc in next 2 sts, dc in next 2 sts, tr in next 2 sts, dc in next 2 sts, hdc in next st, sc in next st; turn = 70 sts

Row 3: (WS) Ch 1, sc in first st, hdc in next st, dc in next 2 sts, tr in next 2 sts, dc in next 2 sts, hdc in next 2 sts, sc in next 2 sts, [hdc in next 2 sts, dc in next 2 sts, tr in next 2 sts, dc in next 2 sts, hdc in next 2 sts, sc in next 2 sts] 4 times, hdc in next 2 sts, dc in next 2 sts, tr in next 2 sts, dc in next 2 sts, hdc in next st, sc in next st; change to **CC4** and turn = 70 sts

Row 4: (RS) With **CC4**, ch 1, sc in first st, sc in next 69 sts; turn = 70 sts

Row 5: (WS) Ch 1, sc in first st, sc in next 69 sts; change to **CC3** and turn = 70 sts

Row 6: (RS) With **CC3**, ch 3 (counts as first dc now and throughout), skip first st, dc in next st, hdc in next 2 sts, [sc in next 2 sts, hdc in next 2 sts, dc in next 2 sts, tr in next 2 sts, dc in next 2 sts, hdc in next 2 sts] 5 times, sc in next 2 sts, hdc in next 2 sts, dc in next 2 sts; turn = 70 sts

BLANKET CHART

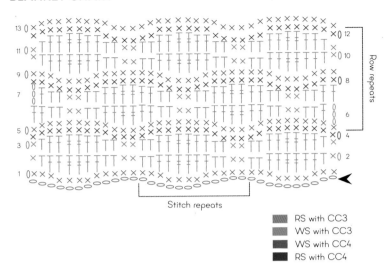

Stitch repeats

Row repeats

- RS with CC3
- WS with CC3
- WS with CC4
- RS with CC4

Row 7: (WS) Ch 3, skip first st, dc in next st, hdc in next 2 sts, sc in next 2 sts, [hdc in next 2 sts, dc in next 2 sts, tr in next 2 sts, dc in next 2 sts, hdc in next 2 sts, sc in next 2 sts] 5 times, hdc in next 2 sts, dc in next 2 sts; change to **CC4** and turn = 70 sts

Rows 8-9: Repeat Rows 4-5

Rows 10-12: Repeat Rows 2-4

Rows 13-60: Repeat Rows 5-12 in established pattern until the blanket is visually square, ending after Row 12. Break off **CC3**

Edge: With **CC4**, ch 1, *sc in next 2 sts, picot, repeat from * around, placing 3 sc in each corner for increasing; join

Fasten off and weave in the ends, wet block the blanket (see General Techniques: Blocking).

BODY WITH LEGS

Make 1. Work in spiral rounds with a 6mm (J) hook and 2 strands of **MC**.

To beg: Ch 3, sl st in third ch from hook to form a ring (or start with a magic ring)

Rnd 1: Ch 1 (does not count as a st), 6 sc in ring, do not join now and throughout = 6 sts

Rnd 2: 2 sc in first st of previous rnd, 2 sc in next 5 sts = 12 sts

Rnd 3: [Sc in next st, 2 sc in next st] 6 times = 18 sts

Rnd 4: [Sc in next 2 sts, 2 sc in next st] 6 times = 24 sts

Rnd 5: [Sc in next 3 sts, 2 sc in next st] 6 times = 30 sts

Rnds 6-8: Sc in each st around = 30 sts

Legs: Sl st in next st, [ch 7, sc in second ch from hook, sc in next 5 chs, sc in next 2 sts of body] 3 times, sc in next 6 sts, [ch 7, sc in second ch from hook, sc in next 5 chs, sc in next 2 sts of body] 2 times, ch 7, sc in second ch from hook, sc in next 5 chs, sl st in next st of body, leave the remaining stitches unworked and mark them as "Front" = 6 legs

Fasten off, leaving a long tail for sewing.

PINCERS

Make 2. Work in rows with a 6mm (J) hook and 2 strands of **MC**.

To beg: Ch 8

Row 1: (WS) Sc in second ch from hook (the skipped ch does not count as a st), sc in next 2 chs, 3 sc in next ch, sc in next 3 chs; turn = 9 sts

Row 2: (RS) Ch 1 (does not count as a st), 3 sc in first st, sc in next 3 sts, ch 9, dc in fourth ch from hook, dc in next 5 chs, skip next st of Row 1, sc in next 3 sts, 3 sc in next st = 18 sts

Fasten off and weave in the ends.

EYELIDS

Make 2. Work in spiral rounds with a 3.75mm (F) hook and 1 strand of **MC**.

To beg: Ch 3, sl st in third ch from hook to form a ring (or start with a magic ring)

Rnd 1: Ch 1 (does not count as a st), 6 sc in ring, do not join now and throughout = 6 sts

Rnd 2: Sc in first st of previous rnd, 2 sc in next st, [sc in next st, 2 sc in next st] 2 times = 9 sts

Rnd 3: [Sc in next 2 sts, 2 sc in next st] 3 times = 12 sts

Rnd 4: [Sc in next 3 sts, 2 sc in next st] 3 times = 15 sts

Rnd 5: [Sc in next 4 sts, 2 sc in next st] 3 times = 18 sts

Sl st in next st, fasten off, leaving a long tail for sewing.

EYESTALKS

Make 2. Work in spiral rounds with a 3.75mm (F) hook and 1 strand of yarn, changing colors (**CC2** and **MC**) as indicated in the pattern.

To beg: With **CC2**, ch 3, sl st in third ch from hook to form a ring (or start with a magic ring)

Rnd 1: Ch 1 (does not count as a st), 6 sc in ring, do not join now and throughout = 6 sts

Rnd 2: 2 sc in first st of previous rnd, sc in next st, [2 sc in next st, sc in next st] 2 times = 9 sts

Rnds 3-4: Sc in each st around = 9 sts

Rnd 5: [Sc in next st, sc2tog] 3 times, change to **MC**, break off **CC2** = 6 sts

Rnd 6: With **MC**, sl st in next st, ch 1, sc in same st as sl st, sc in next 5 sts = 6 sts

Rnds 7-8: Sc in first st of previous rnd, sc in next 5 sts = 6 sts

Sl st in next st, fasten off, leaving a long tail for sewing. Stuff eyestalks.

ASSEMBLING EYESTALKS

Thread the needle with a single strand of **CC1** and stitch a French knot on the front of each eyestalk (1 and 2). Finish off and weave the ends into the inside of the eyestalk.

Position the eyelids on the top of the eyestalks, covering the back side and backstitch around using **MC** (3).

Use a chopstick or a knitting needle for stuffing eyestalks.

PINCER CHART

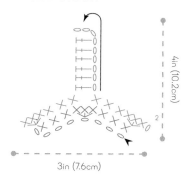

4in (10.2cm)

2

3in (7.6cm)

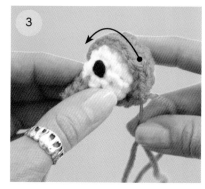

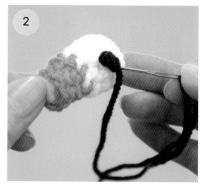

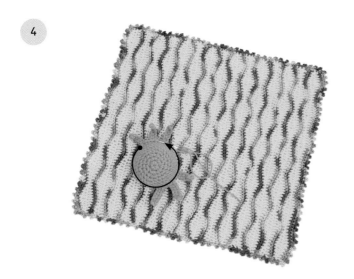

ASSEMBLING SECURITY BLANKET

With RS facing, position the body on the blanket as you like. Whipstitch around the edge of the body with **MC**, leaving an opening at the end for stuffing (4). Do not sew around the edges of the legs.

Stuff body and complete sewing (5).

Place the pincers right up against the front edge of the body and whipstitch across the corresponding edges using **MC** (6). Do not sew around the edges of the pincers.

Position the eyestalks on the top of the body, leaving 1 round space between them (7). Whipstitch each eyestalk around the edge using **MC**.

Thread the needle with a single strand of **CC1** and chain stitch a crooked smile below the right eye (8).

TOPS THE DINOSAUR

Rug, Pillow and Book Bag

Welcome to the majestic world of dinosaurs! These mysterious living creatures inhabited our planet a long time ago, but they are still the most attractive and noble animals loved by everyone. What happened to all of the dinosaurs? Any child would enjoy a bedtime story to discover the answers to all of their dinosaur questions!

Create a unique prehistoric bedroom by decorating it with this triceratops set. The matching rug, pillow and book bag will make bedtime full of lasting memories.

DINOSAUR RUG

SKILL LEVEL

  ○ ○

FINISHED SIZE
39in x 34½in (99cm x 87.6cm)

HOOKS
5.5mm (I), 9mm (M/N)

YARN WEIGHT
4

NUMBER OF STRANDS
1, 2 and 3

**GAUGE WITH 3 STRANDS
AND 9MM (M/N) HOOK**
9 dc x 4.5 rows = 4in x 4in (10cm x 10cm)

STITCH SUMMARY
Ch, sl st, sc, beg sc, hdc,
dc, dc3tog, picot, join

SKILLS
Working in rows and in the round,
working across the bottom of
the foundation chain, sewing

LEFT-HANDED CROCHET
Fully compatible

YARN

Abbreviation	Color	Amount
MC	Forest Green	1093-1312yd (1000-1200m)
CC1	Soft Taupe	218-273yd (200-250m)
CC2	Camo	218-273yd (200-250m)
CC3	Gold (optional)	93-109yd (85-100m)
CC4	Coffee	Small amount
CC5	Natural White	93-109yd (85-100m)

HEAD

Make 1. Work in the round with a 9mm (M/N) hook and 3 strands of **MC**.

NOTE: Ch-2 sps are not included in the total stitch count.

To beg: Ch 3, sl st in third ch from hook to form a ring (or start with a magic ring)

Rnd 1: Ch 2 (does not count as a st now and throughout), 12 dc in ring; join = 12 sts

Rnd 2: Ch 2, 2 dc in same st as join, 2 dc in next 11 sts; join = 24 sts

Rnd 3: Ch 2, dc in same st as join, 2 dc in next st, [dc in next st, 2 dc in next st] 11 times; join = 36 sts

Rnd 4: Ch 2, 2 dc in same st as join, dc in next 2 sts, [2 dc in next st, dc in next 2 sts] 11 times; join = 48 sts

Rnd 5: Ch 2, dc in same st as join, dc in next 2 sts, 2 dc in next st, [dc in next 3 sts, 2 dc in next st] 11 times; join = 60 sts

Rnd 6: Ch 2, 2 dc in same st as join, dc in next 4 sts, [2 dc in next st, dc in next 4 sts] 11 times; join = 72 sts

Rnd 7: Ch 2, dc in same st as join, dc in next 4 sts, 2 dc in next st, [dc in next 5 sts, 2 dc in next st] 11 times; join = 84 sts

Rnd 8: Ch 2, 2 dc in same st as join, dc in next 6 sts, [2 dc in next st, dc in next 6 sts] 11 times; join = 96 sts

Rnd 9: Ch 2, dc in same st as join, dc in next 6 sts, 2 dc in next st, [dc in next 7 sts, 2 dc in next st] 11 times; join = 108 sts

Rnd 10: Ch 2, 2 dc in same st as join, dc in next 8 sts, [2 dc in next st, dc in next 8 sts] 11 times; join = 120 sts

Rnd 11: Ch 2, dc in same st as join, dc in next 8 sts, 2 dc in next st, [dc in next 9 sts, 2 dc in next st] 11 times; join = 132 sts

Rnd 12: Ch 2, 2 dc in same st as join, dc in next 15 sts, (2 dc, ch 2, 2 dc) in next st, [dc in next 10 sts, (2 dc, ch 2, 2 dc) in next st] 8 times, dc in next 5 sts, [2 dc in next st, dc in next 10 sts] 2 times; join = 162 sts

Rnd 13: Ch 2, dc in same st as join, dc in next 10 sts, 2 dc in next st, skip st, dc in next 6 sts, (2 dc, ch 2, 2 dc) in next ch-2 sp, dc in next 6 sts, [skip 2 sts, dc in next 6 sts, (2 dc, ch 2, 2 dc) in next ch-2 sp, dc in next 6 sts] 8 times, skip st, [dc in next 11 sts, 2 dc in next st] 2 times; join = 183 sts

Rnd 14: Ch 2, 2 dc in same st as join, dc in next 12 sts, skip st, dc in next 7 sts, (2 dc, ch 2, 2 dc) in next ch-2 sp, dc in next 7 sts, [skip 2 sts, dc in next 7 sts, (2 dc, ch 2, 2 dc) in next ch-2 sp, dc in next 7 sts] 8 times, skip st, [2 dc in next st, dc in next 12 sts] 2 times; join = 204 sts

Rnd 15: Ch 2, dc in same st as join, dc in next 12 sts, 2 dc in next st, skip st, dc in next 8 sts, (2 dc, ch 2, 2 dc) in next ch-2 sp, dc in next 8 sts, [skip 2 sts, dc in next 8 sts, (2 dc, ch 2, 2 dc) in next ch-2 sp, dc in next 8 sts] 8 times, skip st, [dc in next 13 sts, 2 dc in next st] 2 times; join = 225 sts

Rnd 16: Ch 2, 2 dc in same st as join, dc in next 14 sts, skip st, dc in next 9 sts, (2 dc, ch 2, 2 dc) in next ch-2 sp, dc in next 9 sts, [skip 2 sts, dc in next 9 sts, (2 dc, ch 2, 2 dc) in next ch-2 sp, dc in next 9 sts] 8 times, skip st, [2 dc in next st, dc in next 14 sts] 2 times; join = 246 sts

Rnd 17: Ch 2, dc in same st as join, dc in next 14 sts, 2 dc in next st, skip st, dc in next 10 sts, (2 dc, ch 2, 2 dc) in next ch-2 sp, dc in next 10 sts, [skip 2 sts, dc in next 10 sts, (2 dc, ch 2, 2 dc) in next ch-2 sp, dc in next 10 sts] 8 times, skip st, [dc in next 15 sts, 2 dc in next st] 2 times; join = 267 sts

Skip 29 sts and place **Marker A** in next ch-2 sp, fasten off and weave in the ends. Continue to work edging with a 9mm (M/N) hook and 3 strands of **CC2**.

Edge: (RS) Beg sc in sp with **Marker A** and remove the marker, (picot, sc) in same sp, sc in next 11 sts, [skip 2 sts, sc in next 11 sts, (2 sc, picot, sc) in next ch-2 sp, sc in next 11 sts] 7 times, skip 2 sts, sc in next 11 sts, (2 sc, picot) in next ch-2 sp = 201 sts and 9 picots

Fasten off and weave in the ends.

Spray block the head if necessary (see General Techniques: Blocking).

HEAD CHART

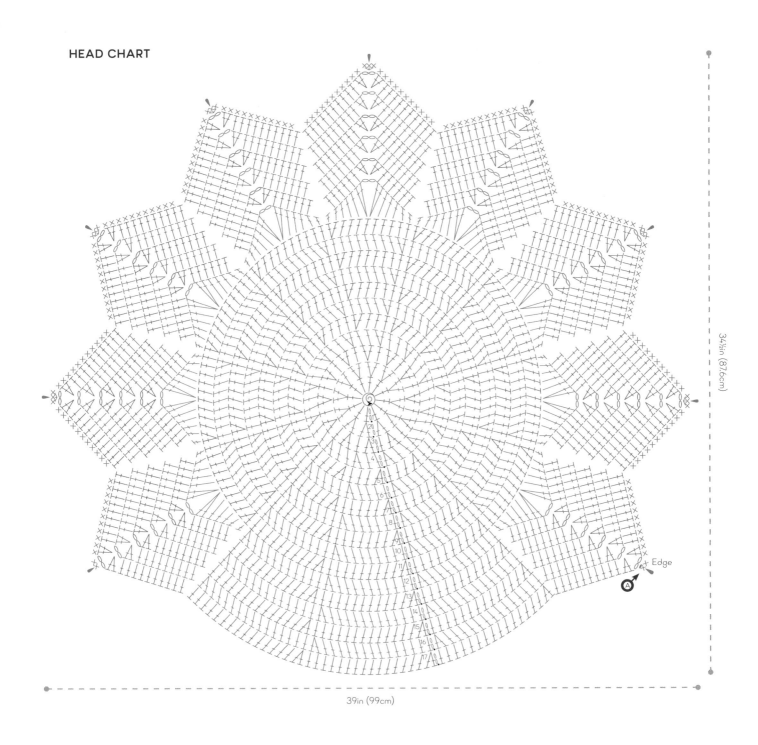

34¼in (876cm)

39in (99cm)

Edge

A

HORN CHART

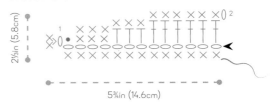

2⅛in (5.8cm)

5¾in (14.6cm)

MUZZLE

Make 1. Work in the round with a 9mm (M/N) hook and 2 strands of **CC1**.

To beg: Ch 29

Rnd 1: Dc in third ch from hook (2 skipped chs do not count as a st), dc in next 25 chs, 6 dc in last ch, continue working across the bottom of the foundation ch, dc in next 25 chs, 5 dc in last ch; join = 62 sts

Rnd 2: Ch 2 (does not count as a st now and throughout), 2 dc in same st as join, dc in next 12 sts, 3 dc in next st (**bottom point**), dc in next 12 sts, 2 dc in next 6 sts, dc in next 11 sts, dc3tog (**center top**), dc in next 11 sts, 2 dc in next 5 sts; join = 74 sts

Rnd 3: Ch 2, 2 dc in same st as join, dc in next 14 sts, 3 dc in next st (**bottom point**), dc in next 13 sts, [dc in next st, 2 dc in next st] 6 times, dc in next 10 sts, dc3tog (**center top**), dc in next 10 sts, [2 dc in next st, dc in next st] 5 times; join = 86 sts

Rnd 4: Ch 2, dc in same st as join, dc in next st, 2 dc in next st, dc in next 14 sts, 3 dc in next st (**bottom point**), dc in next 14 sts, [2 dc in next st, dc in next 2 sts] 6 times, dc in next 9 sts, dc3tog (**center top**), dc in next 9 sts, [dc in next 2 sts, 2 dc in next st] 5 times; join = 98 sts

Rnd 5: Ch 2, 2 dc in same st as join, dc in next 18 sts, 3 dc in next st (**bottom point**), dc in next 15 sts, [dc in next 3 sts, 2 dc in next st] 6 times, dc in next 8 sts, dc3tog (**center top**), dc in next 8 sts, [2 dc in next st, dc in next 3 sts] 5 times; join = 110 sts

Fasten off, leaving a long tail for sewing.

MUZZLE CHART

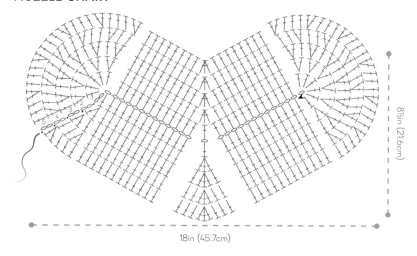

8½in (21.6cm)

18in (45.7cm)

HORNS

Make 3. Work in rows with a 9mm (M/N) hook and 2 strands of **CC5**.

To beg: Ch 14

Row 1: (WS) Sl st in second ch from hook (the skipped ch does not count as a st), sc in next 3 chs, hdc in next 3 chs, dc in next 6 chs; turn = 13 sts

Row 2: (RS) Ch 1 (does not count as a st), sc in next 13 sts, 2 sc in end ch, continue working across the bottom of the foundation ch, sc in next 13 sts = 28 sts

Fasten off, leaving a long single strand of **CC5** for sewing. Weave in the other ends.

EYES

Make 2. Follow the instructions for the basic eyes (see Common Shapes: Basic Eyes). Use 2 strands of **CC4** with a 9mm (M/N) hook for the pupils and 1 strand of **CC5** with a 5.5mm (I) hook for the highlights.

Use stitch markers to mark the **bottom point** and the **center top** of the muzzle.

BOW (OPTIONAL)

Make 1. Follow the instructions for the big bow using **CC3** (see Common Shapes: Big Bow).

ASSEMBLING RUG

With RS facing, place the muzzle onto the head so that the pointy edge of the muzzle is 1 round above the bottom edge of the head. Backstitch around the muzzle edge using the long **CC1** tail from the muzzle (1).

Place the first horn right up against the muzzle, centering it at the top edge. Using the long **CC5** tail from the horn, whipstitch across the bottom edge and backstitch around the remaining edge of the horn (1).

Position the other 2 horns on each side of the head with the top 3 spikes of the head between the horns (1). The tips of the horns should extend beyond the head edge by approximately 2in (5cm). Using **CC5**, whipstitch across the bottom edge and backstitch around the remaining edge of the horns, leaving the tips of the horns unstitched (2).

Place the eyes on each side above the muzzle and backstitch around using the long **CC4** tail from the eyes (3).

If using, place the bow onto the head, covering the bottom edge of the left horn (optional) and backstitch around the center of the bow using **CC3** (4). Keep the side edges of the bow unattached or whipstitch the corners to keep them in place.

If desired, make a removable non-slip lining (see General Techniques: Non-Slip Lining).

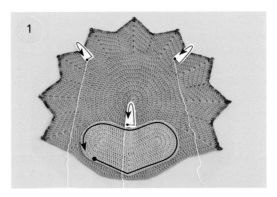

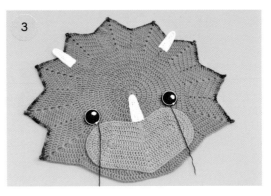

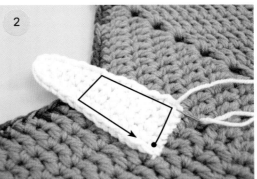

DINOSAUR PILLOW

SKILL LEVEL

FINISHED SIZE
17½in (44.5cm) diameter

HOOKS
3.75mm (F), 4.25mm (G),
5mm (H), 5.5mm (I)

YARN WEIGHT
4

NUMBER OF STRANDS
1

GAUGE WITH 1 STRAND
AND 5.5MM (I) HOOK
14 sc x 16 rows = 4in x 4in (10cm x 10cm)

STITCH SUMMARY
Ch, sl st, sc, beg sc, sc3tog,
hdc, dc, dc3tog, tr, picot, join

SKILLS
Working in rows and in the round,
working across the bottom of the
foundation chain, blocking, sewing

LEFT-HANDED CROCHET
Fully compatible

YARN

Abbreviation	Color	Amount
MC	Forest Green	93-109yd (85-100m)
CC2	Camo	185-251yd (170-230m)
CC3	Gold	273-328yd (250-300m)

All other contrasting colors are the same as for
the Dinosaur Rug (small amount of each).

PILLOW BASE

Make 1 front and 1 back using 1 strand of **CC3** with a 5.5mm (I) hook. Follow the instructions for the round pillow base (see Common Shapes: Round Pillow Base). Fasten off after finishing each piece.

Holding the front and the back pieces together with WS facing each other, work Rnd 26 through both pieces of fabric at the same time using 1 strand of **CC2**.

Rnd 26: Beg sc in same st as previous sl st, sc in next 140 sts, stuff the pillow, sc in next 15 sts; join = 156 sts

Rnd 27: Ch 9, dc in third ch from hook, 2 dc in next 6 chs (first spiral made), skip st with join, skip next 2 sts of Rnd 26, sl st in next st, *ch 9, dc in third ch from hook, 2 dc in next 6 chs (next spiral made), skip 2 sts of Rnd 26, sl st in next st**, repeat around from * to ** (1) = 52 spirals

Fasten off and weave in the ends.

HEAD

Make 1. Work in the round with a 3.75mm (F) hook and 1 strand of **MC**.

NOTE: Ch-2 sps are not included in the total stitch count.

To beg: Ch 3, sl st in third ch from hook to form a ring (or start with a magic ring)

Rnd 1: Ch 2 (does not count as a st now and throughout), 12 dc in ring; join = 12 sts

Rnd 2: Ch 2, 2 dc in same st as join, 2 dc in next 11 sts; join = 24 sts

Rnd 3: Ch 2, dc in same st as join, 2 dc in next st, [dc in next st, 2 dc in next st] 11 times; join = 36 sts

HEAD CHART

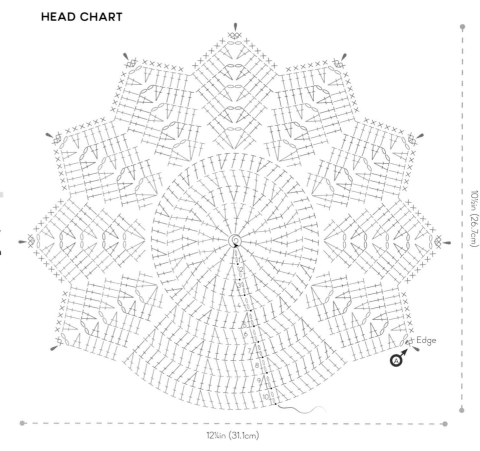

10½in (26.7cm)

12¼in (31.1cm)

Edge

Rnd 4: Ch 2, 2 dc in same st as join, dc in next 2 sts, [2 dc in next st, dc in next 2 sts] 11 times, join = 48 sts

Rnd 5: Ch 2, dc in same st as join, dc in next 2 sts, 2 dc in next st, [dc in next 3 sts, 2 dc in next st] 11 times; join = 60 sts

Rnd 6: Ch 2, 2 dc in same st as join, dc in next 4 sts, skip st, dc in next st, (2 dc, ch 2, 2 dc) in next st, dc in next st, [skip 2 sts, dc in next st, (2 dc, ch 2, 2 dc) in next st, dc in next st] 8 times, skip st, [2 dc in next st, dc in next 4 sts] 2 times; join = 72 sts

Rnd 7: Ch 2, dc in same st as join, dc in next 4 sts, 2 dc in next st, skip st, dc in next 2 sts, (2 dc, ch 2, 2 dc) in next ch-2 sp, dc in next 2 sts, [skip 2 sts, dc in next 2 sts, (2 dc, ch 2, 2 dc) in next ch-2 sp, dc in next 2 sts] 8 times, skip st, [dc in next 5 sts, 2 dc in next st] 2 times; join = 93 sts

Rnd 8: Ch 2, 2 dc in same st as join, dc in next 6 sts, skip st, dc in next 3 sts, (2 dc, ch 2, 2 dc) in next ch-2 sp, dc in next 3 sts, [skip 2 sts, dc in next 3 sts, (2 dc, ch 2, 2 dc) in next ch-2 sp, dc in next 3 sts] 8 times, skip st, [2 dc in next st, dc in next 6 sts] 2 times; join = 114 sts

Rnd 9: Ch 2, dc in same st as join, dc in next 6 sts, 2 dc in next st, skip st, dc in next 4 sts, (2 dc, ch 2, 2 dc) in next ch-2 sp, dc in next 4 sts, [skip 2 sts, dc in next 4 sts, (2 dc, ch 2, 2 dc) in next ch-2 sp, dc in next 4 sts] 8 times, skip st, [dc in next 7 sts, 2 dc in next st] 2 times; join = 135 sts

Rnd 10: Ch 2, 2 dc in same st as join, dc in next 8 sts, skip st, dc in next 5 sts, (2 dc, ch 2, 2 dc) in next ch-2 sp, dc in next 5 sts, [skip 2 sts, dc in next 5 sts, (2 dc, ch 2, 2 dc) in next ch-2 sp, dc in next 5 sts] 8 times, skip st, [2 dc in next st, dc in next 8 sts] 2 times; join = 156 sts

Skip 17 sts and place **Marker A** in next ch-2 sp, fasten off, leaving a long **MC** tail for sewing. Continue to work edging with a 3.75mm (F) hook and 1 strand of **CC2** as follows:

Edge: (RS) Beg sc in sp with **Marker A** and remove the marker, (picot, sc) in same sp, sc in next 6 sts, [skip 2 sts, sc in next 6 sts, (2 sc, picot, sc) in next ch-2 sp, sc in next 6 sts] 7 times, skip 2 sts, sc in next 6 sts, (2 sc, picot) in next ch-2 sp = 121 sts and 9 picots

Fasten off and weave in the ends. Wet block the head (see General Techniques: Blocking).

MUZZLE CHART

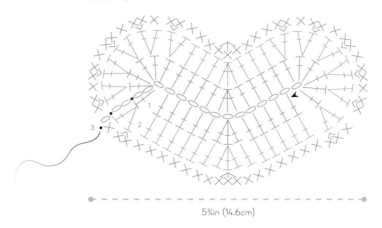

5¾in (14.6cm)

SHORT HORN CHART

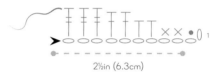

2½in (6.3cm)

MUZZLE

Make 1. Work in the round with a 5mm (H) hook and 1 strand of **CC1**.

To beg: Ch 15

Rnd 1: Dc in third ch from hook (2 skipped chs do not count as a st), dc in next 5 chs, 3 dc in next ch, dc in next 5 chs, 6 dc in last ch, continue working across the bottom of the foundation ch, dc in next 4 chs, dc3tog, dc in next 4 chs, 5 dc in last ch; join = 34 sts

Rnd 2 Ch 2 (does not count as a st), 2 dc in same st as join, dc in next 6 sts, 3 dc in next st, dc in next 6 sts, 2 dc in next 6 sts, dc in next 3 sts, dc3tog, dc in next 3 sts, 2 dc in next 5 sts; join = 46 sts

Rnd 3: Ch 1 (does not count as a st), sc in same st as join, 2 sc in next st, sc in next 7 sts, 3 sc in next st, sc in next 7 sts, [2 sc in next st, sc in next st] 6 times, sc in next 2 sts, sc3tog, sc in next 3 sts, 2 sc in next st, [sc in next st, 2 sc in next st] 4 times; join = 58 sts

Fasten off, leaving a long tail for sewing. Weave in the end from the beg.

SHORT HORN

Make 1. Work in rows with a 4.25mm (G) hook and 1 strand of **CC5**.

To beg: Ch 11

Row 1: (RS) Sl st in second ch from hook (the skipped ch does not count as a st), sc in next 2 chs, hdc in next 2 chs, dc in next 2 chs, tr in next 3 chs = 10 sts

Fasten off, leaving a long tail for sewing. Weave in the end from the beg.

LONG HORNS

Make 2. Follow the instructions for the horns in Dinosaur Rug (see Dinosaur Rug: Horns). Use a 4.25mm (G) hook and 1 strand of **CC5**.

EYES

Make 2. Follow the instructions for the basic eyes (see Common Shapes: Basic Eyes). Use 1 strand of **CC4** with a 4.25mm (G) hook for the pupils and 1 strand of **CC5** for the highlights.

ASSEMBLING PILLOW

Place the head onto the front of the pillow and backstitch around using the long **MC** tail from the head (2).

Position the muzzle so that the pointy edge of the muzzle is just above the bottom edge of the head. Backstitch around the edge of the muzzle using the long **CC1** tail from the muzzle (3).

Position the 2 long horns on each side of the head with the top 3 spikes of the head between the horns. The tips of the horns should extend beyond the edge of the head by approximately 1½in (3.8cm). Using the long **CC5** tail from the horns, whipstitch across the bottom edge and backstitch around the remaining edge of the horns (3).

Place the short horn right up against the muzzle, centering it at the top edge. Using the long **CC5** tail from the horn, whipstitch across the bottom edge and backstitch around the remaining edge of the horn (4).

Place the eyes on each side right up against the muzzle and backstitch around using the long **CC4** tail from the eyes (4).

If desired, make a small bow using 1 strand of **CC3** (see Common Shapes: Small Bow). Place the bow onto the head, covering the bottom edge of the left long horn and backstitch around the center of the bow using **CC3**.

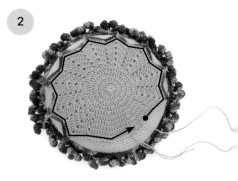

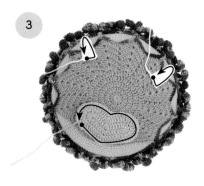

Make the pillow even more fun by adding a dinosaur head on the back as well.

DINOSAUR BOOK BAG

SKILL LEVEL

FINISHED SIZE
12¾in x 12¼in (32.4cm x 31.1cm)

HOOKS
3.75mm (F), 4.25mm (G), 5mm (H)

YARN WEIGHT
4

NUMBER OF STRANDS
1

**GAUGE WITH 1 STRAND
AND 5MM (H) HOOK**
15 dc x 8 rows = 4in x 4in (10cm x 10cm)

STITCH SUMMARY
Ch, sl st, sc, beg sc, sc3tog, hdc,
dc, dc3tog, tr, cluster, picot, join

SKILLS
Working in rows and in the round,
working across the bottom of
the foundation chain, changing
colors, blocking, sewing

LEFT-HANDED CROCHET
Fully compatible

YARN

Abbreviation	Color	Amount
MC	Forest Green	93-109yd (85-100m)
CC3	Gold	93-109yd (85-100m)
CC4	Coffee	93-109yd (85-100m)
CC6	Pumpkin	93-109yd (85-100m)

All other contrasting colors are the same as for
the Dinosaur Rug (small amount of each).

BOOK BAG

Make 1. Work in the round with a 5mm (H) hook and 1 strand of yarn, changing colors (**CC4**, **CC3** and **CC6**) in every round. Begin with **CC4**.

To beg: Ch 43

Rnd 1: Dc in third ch from hook (2 skipped chs do not count as a st), dc in next 39 chs, 3 dc in last ch, continue working across the bottom of the foundation ch, dc in next 39 chs, 2 dc in last ch; join = 84 sts

Rnd 2: (Ch 3, 2 dc) in same st as join (counts as beg cluster now and throughout), skip 2 sts, [3 dc in next st, skip 2 sts] 27 times, sl st in top of beg ch-3 = 28 clusters

Rnds 3-25: (Ch 3, 2 dc) in same sp between clusters, [skip cluster, 3 dc in next sp between clusters] 27 times, sl st in top of beg ch-3 = 28 clusters

Check the bag length, add or omit rounds if alterations are needed. Change to **CC2** and break off all other colors.

Rnds 26-27: With **CC2**, ch 1 (does not count as a st now and throughout), sc in same st as join, sc in next 83 sts; join = 84 sts

Fasten off and weave in the ends.

TIES

Holding the bag flat, mark 6 stitches on each side of the bag by placing a stitch marker in first and sixth stitches (1).

Work with a 5mm (H) hook and 1 strand of **CC2**.

To beg: (RS) Ch 60, sc across 6 marked sts on one side of the bag, ch 62, turn = 6 sts and 2 long ch-tails (2)

Row 1: (WS) Dc in third ch from hook (2 skipped chs count as first dc), 2 dc in next 6 chs, sc in next 53 chs, sc in next 6 sts, sc in next 53 chs, 2 dc in next 7 chs = 140 sts

Fasten off and weave in the ends. Finish the second tie in the same manner.

DINOSAUR

Make the head, muzzle, horns and eyes following the instructions in Dinosaur Pillow (see Dinosaur Pillow: Head, Dinosaur Pillow: Muzzle, Dinosaur Pillow: Horns and Dinosaur Pillow: Eyes).

ASSEMBLING BOOK BAG

Holding the bag flat, place the head onto the bag and backstitch around using the long **MC** tail from the head (3).

Sew all the other parts (4) in the same way as for Dinosaur Pillow (see Dinosaur Pillow: Assembling Pillow).

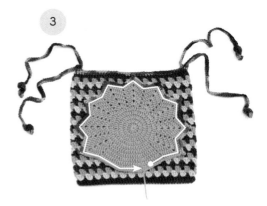

USEFUL INFORMATION

CROCHET TERMINOLOGY

The patterns featured in this book are written using abbreviations in American crochet terms. Please use the comparison chart below to convert the patterns to British terminology if needed.

Abbreviation	Symbol	American (US) Term	British (UK) Term
Ch	o	Chain	Chain
Sl st	•	Slip stitch	Slip stitch
Sc	×	Single crochet	Double crochet
Hdc	T	Half double crochet	Half treble crochet
Dc	⊤	Double crochet	Treble crochet
Tr	⊤	Treble crochet	Double treble crochet
		Skip	Miss
		Gauge	Tension

ABBREVIATIONS

This table explains all of the standard abbreviations and symbols used in this book.

Abbreviation	Symbol	Description in US Terms
Arch	⌒ 5	**Arch** is a group of 3 or more chains as indicated in the pattern; when working in arch, insert the hook under the arch (and not into a specific chain), unless otherwise stated
Beg		Begin(ning)

Abbreviation	Symbol	Description in US Terms
Beg dc	I	**Beginning (standing) double crochet** – Make a slipknot and keep the loop on the hook, yo, insert the hook through the stitch and complete dc as normal
Beg PC	(popcorn symbol)	**Beginning popcorn stitch** – Ch 3 (counts as dc), 4 dc in same st, remove the hook from the loop and insert hook from front to back through the top of beg ch-3, replace the loop onto the hook (from the last dc) and pull it through
Beg sc	x	**Beginning (standing) single crochet** – Make a slipknot and keep the loop on the hook, insert the hook through the stitch and complete sc as normal
Bpsc	ʇ	**Back post single crochet** – Insert the hook from back to front to back around the post of the stitch, yo and pull up a loop, yo and pull yarn through 2 loops on the hook
CC		Contrasting color (might be indicated by a number)
Ch(s)	o	**Chain(s)** – Yo and pull through the loop on the hook
Ch-		Indicates a number of chains or spaces previously made (example: ch-2 sp)

Abbreviation	Symbol	Description in US Terms
Cluster		**Cluster** – 3 dc in same space
Cm		Centimeter(s)
Crest		**Crest** is a combination of stitches worked across the shell – Dc in first st of the shell, [dc in next st, picot] 7 times, dc in last st = 9 dc and 7 picots
Dc		**Double crochet** – Yo, insert the hook in stitch, yo and pull up a loop, [yo and pull through 2 loops] 2 times
Dc2(3)tog		**Double crochet 2 (3) together (decrease)** – [Yo, insert the hook in next stitch, yo and pull up a loop, yo and pull through 2 loops] 2 (3) times, yo and pull through all loops on the hook (1 stitch made)
		2 (3) dc in same stitch or space
		Direction indicators
Fasten off		Cut working yarn, draw the end through the loop on the hook and pull up tight

Abbreviation	Symbol	Description in US Terms
FDC	⌐ɔ	**Double crochet in front of work** – Yo, insert the hook under both loops of sc two rows below and complete dc as normal, leaving the two rows of ch-2 sps in the back unworked
Fpsc	⌠	**Front post single crochet** – Insert the hook from front to back to front around the post of the stitch, yo and pull up a loop, yo and pull yarn through 2 loops on the hook
Hdc	T	**Half double crochet** – Yo, insert the hook in stitch, yo and pull up a loop, yo and pull through all loops on the hook
	V	2 hdc in same stitch or space
In		Inch(es)
Join		Sl st in top of the first stitch (not a ch)
M		Meter(s)
	◎	Magic ring or ch-3 circle
Marker	⬤➤	Stitch marker (indicated by a letter)

Abbreviation	Symbol	Description in US Terms
MC		Main color
OS		**Open shell** – (2 dc, ch 1, 2 dc) in same space
OS over shell		Work OS in ch-1 sp (the center) of open shell below
PC		**Popcorn stitch** – 5 dc in stitch indicated in the pattern, remove the hook from the loop and insert it from front to back through the top of the first dc, replace the loop onto the hook (from the last dc) and pull it through
Picot		**Picot** – Ch 3, insert the hook from right to left under the front loop and bottom vertical bar of previously made stitch (the base of the stitch), yo and pull through all loops on the hook
Rnd(s)		**Round**(s) – Work in spiral or join the rounds, as indicated in the pattern
Row(s)		**Row**(s) – Turn after finishing each row, as indicated in the pattern
RS		Right side (front side of the item)

Abbreviation	Symbol	Description in US Terms
Rsc	⌇⤬	**Reverse single crochet (crab stitch)** – Insert the hook in stitch to the right from front to back, yo and pull it through, yo and pull through all loops on the hook (see Crochet Techniques: Left-Handed Crochet for left-handed conversion)
Sc	✕	**Single crochet** – Insert the hook in stitch, yo and pull up a loop, yo and pull through all loops on the hook
Sc2(3)tog	⤬⤬ ⤬⤬⤬	**Single crochet 2 (3) together (decrease)** – [Insert the hook in next stitch, yo and pull up a loop] 2 (3) times, yo and pull through all loops on the hook (1 stitch made)
	⤬⤬ ⤬⤬⤬	2 (3) sc in same stitch or space
		Seam

Abbreviation	Symbol	Description in US Terms
Shell		**Shell** – 6 or more stitches worked in same space
Slipknot		**Slipknot** – Twist the end of working yarn to form a loop, insert the hook through the loop, yo and draw working yarn through the loop, pull the end to tighten the knot and adjust the size of the loop on the hook
Sl st	•	**Slip stitch** – Insert the hook in stitch, yo and pull through the stitch and loop on the hook
Sp		**Space** is a gap created by one or more chains; it might also be a space between two stitches or groups of stitches. Insert the hook into a chain space or in a space between stitches (not a specific chain or stitch)
St(s)		**Stitch**(es)
Tr		**Treble crochet** – Yo twice, insert the hook in stitch, yo and pull up a loop, [yo and pull through 2 loops] 3 times

Abbreviation	Symbol	Description in US Terms
	⑂	2 tr in same stitch or space
WS		Wrong side (back side of the item)
Yd		Yard(s)
Yo		Yarn over hook
	~	Yarn tail left for sewing
[ ]		Work the instructions written within brackets as many times as indicated after brackets
( )		Parentheses are used in explanations or to indicate a group of stitches
* or **		Asterisks are used as reference marks
=		Equal sign indicates the total stitch count at the end of the row/rnd

COMMON SHAPES

BASIC EYES

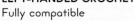

FINISHED SIZE
Varies depending
on pattern

HOOK
See pattern

YARN WEIGHT
4

NUMBER OF STRANDS
See pattern

GAUGE
Varies, depending
on pattern

STITCH SUMMARY
Ch, sl st, sc, join

SKILLS
Working in the round,
sewing

LEFT-HANDED CROCHET
Fully compatible

PUPILS

Make 2. Work in the round using
the suggested yarn and hook for the
specific pattern.

To beg: Ch 3, sl st in third ch from
hook to form a ring (or start with a
magic ring)

Rnd 1: Ch 1 (does not count as a st
now and throughout), 6 sc in ring; join
= 6 sts

Rnd 2: Ch 1, 2 sc in same st as join,
2 sc in next 5 sts; join = 12 sts

Rnd 3: Ch 1, sc in same st as join,
2 sc in next st, [sc in next st, 2 sc in
next st] 5 times; join = 18 sts

Fasten off, leaving a long single
strand of yarn for sewing. Weave in
the other ends.

HIGHLIGHTS

Make 2. Work in the round using
the suggested yarn and hook for the
specific pattern.

To beg: Ch 3, sl st in third ch from
hook to form a ring (or start with a
magic ring)

Rnd 1: Ch 1 (does not count as a st),
6 sc in ring; join = 6 sts

Fasten off, leaving a long single
strand of yarn for sewing. Weave in
the other ends.

ASSEMBLING EYES

Place the highlight on top of the
pupil and backstitch around using the
long tail from the highlight (1). Finish
the second eye in the same manner.

PUPIL CHART

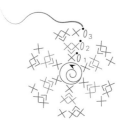

HIGHLIGHT CHART

BOWS

FINISHED SIZE
Big bow: 6¼in x 10¼in
(15.9cm x 26cm)

Small bow: 2¾in x 4in
(7cm x 10.2cm)

HOOK
Big bow: 9mm (M/N)

Small bow: 3.75mm (F)

YARN WEIGHT
4

NUMBER OF STRANDS
1 and 3

GAUGE
Not important

STITCH SUMMARY
Ch, sl st, sc, sc3tog,
PC, beg PC, join

SKILLS
Working in rows and
in the round, sewing

LEFT-HANDED CROCHET
Fully compatible

BIG BOW

Make 1. Begin by working in the round with a 9mm (M/N) hook and 3 strands of yarn, using the recommended color for the specific pattern.

To beg: Ch 3, sl st in third ch from hook to form a ring (or start with a magic ring)

Rnd 1: Ch 1 (does not count as a st now and throughout), 6 sc in ring; join = 6 sts

Rnd 2: Beg PC in same st as join, ch 2, [PC in next st, ch 2] 5 times; join = 6 PC

Rnd 3: Ch 1, [3 sc in next ch-2 sp] 6 times; join = 18 sts

Work the bow sides in rows from now on:

Row 4: (RS) Ch 1, 3 sc in same st as join, [3 sc in next st] 3 times, *skip 5 sts, place **Marker A** in next st**; turn = 12 sts

Rows 5-10: Ch 1, sc in first st, sc in next 11 sts; turn = 12 sts

Fasten off and weave in the ends.

With RS facing you, join 3 strands of yarn in st with **Marker A** leaving a long single strand of yarn at the beginning for sewing. Repeat Rows 4 to 10 and finishing, omitting the instructions from * to **. Remove the marker. To assemble, see Assembling Bow.

SMALL BOW

Make 1. Begin by working in the round with a 3.75mm (F) hook and 1 strand of yarn, using the recommended color for the specific pattern.

To beg: Ch 3, sl st in third ch from hook to form a ring (or start with a magic ring)

Rnd 1: Ch 1 (does not count as a st now and throughout), 6 sc in ring; join = 6 sts

Rnd 2: Beg PC in same st as join, ch 2, [PC in next st, ch 2] 5 times; join = 6 PC

Rnd 3: Ch 1, [3 sc in next ch-2 sp] 6 times; join = 18 sts

Work the bow sides in rows from now on:

Row 4: (RS) Ch 1, 3 sc in same st as join, [3 sc in next st] 3 times, *skip 5 sts, place **Marker A** in next st**; turn = 12 sts

Rows 5-11: Ch 1, sc in first st, sc in next 11 sts; turn = 12 sts

Row 12: Ch 1, do not skip first st, [sc3tog] 4 times = 4 sts

Fasten off, leaving a long tail for sewing. Weave in the other ends.

With RS facing you, join yarn in st with **Marker A**. Repeat Rows 4 to 12 and finishing, omitting the instructions from * to **. Remove the marker. To assemble, see Assembling Bow.

ASSEMBLING BOW

Fold both gathered sides of the bow towards the center on WS and whipstitch across each edge to secure (2). Weave in the end after finishing the first edge but leave a long tail for sewing after finishing second edge.

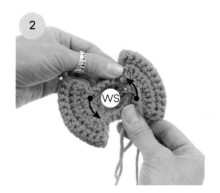

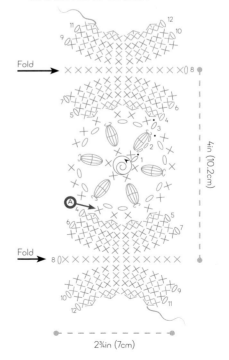

BIG BOW CHART

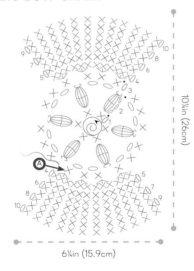

10¼in (26cm)

6¼in (15.9cm)

SMALL BOW CHART

Fold →

Fold →

4in (10.2cm)

2¾in (7cm)

PILLOW BASES

FINISHED SIZE
Round pillow: 13in (33cm) diameter

Oval pillow: 13in x 18½in (33cm x 47cm)

HOOK
5.5mm (I)

YARN WEIGHT
4

NUMBER OF STRANDS
1

GAUGE WITH 1 STRAND AND 5.5MM (I) HOOK
14 sc x 16 rows = 4in x 4in (10cm x 10cm)

STITCH SUMMARY
Ch, sl st, sc

SKILLS
Working in spiral rounds and working across the bottom of the foundation chain

LEFT-HANDED CROCHET
Fully compatible

ROUND PILLOW BASE

Make 1 front and 1 back. Work in spiral rounds with a 5.5mm (I) hook and 1 strand of yarn as recommended for the specific pattern. Use a stitch marker to mark the beginning of each round as you go.

To beg: Ch 3, sl st in third ch from hook to form a ring (or start with a magic ring)

Rnd 1: Ch 1 (does not count as a st), 6 sc in ring, do not join now and throughout = 6 sts

Rnd 2: 2 sc in first st of previous rnd, 2 sc in next 5 sts = 12 sts

Rnd 3: 2 sc in each st around = 24 sts

Rnd 4: Sc in each st around = 24 sts

Rnd 5: [Sc in next st, 2 sc in next st] 12 times = 36 sts

Rnd 6: Sc in each st around = 36 sts

Rnd 7: [Sc in next 2 sts, 2 sc in next st] 12 times = 48 sts

Rnd 8: Sc in each st around = 48 sts

Rnd 9: [Sc in next 3 sts, 2 sc in next st] 12 times = 60 sts

Rnd 10: Sc in each st around = 60 sts

Rnd 11: [Sc in next 4 sts, 2 sc in next st] 12 times = 72 sts

Rnd 12: Sc in each st around = 72 sts

Rnd 13: [Sc in next 5 sts, 2 sc in next st] 12 times = 84 sts

Rnd 14: Sc in each st around = 84 sts

Rnd 15: [Sc in next 6 sts, 2 sc in next st] 12 times = 96 sts

Rnd 16: Sc in each st around = 96 sts

Rnd 17: [Sc in next 7 sts, 2 sc in next st] 12 times = 108 sts

Rnd 18: Sc in each st around = 108 sts

Rnd 19: [Sc in next 8 sts, 2 sc in next st] 12 times = 120 sts

Rnd 20: Sc in each st around = 120 sts

Rnd 21: [Sc in next 9 sts, 2 sc in next st] 12 times = 132 sts

Rnd 22: Sc in each st around = 132 sts

Rnd 23: [Sc in next 10 sts, 2 sc in next st] 12 times = 144 sts

Rnd 24: Sc in each st around = 144 sts

Rnd 25: [Sc in next 11 sts, 2 sc in next st] 12 times = 156 sts

Sl st in next st. Fasten off if indicated in the pattern and check tips for assembling pillow (see Assembling Pillow).

ROUND PILLOW BASE CHART

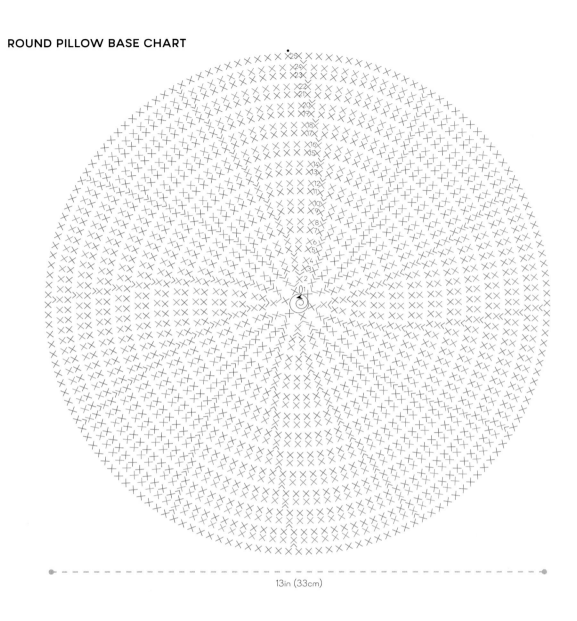

13in (33cm)

OVAL PILLOW BASE

Make 1 front and 1 back. Work in spiral rounds with a 5.5mm (I) hook and 1 strand of yarn as recommended for the specific pattern. Use a stitch marker to mark the beginning of each round as you go.

To beg: Ch 23

Rnd 1: Sc in second ch from hook (the skipped ch does not count as a st), sc in next 20 chs, 3 sc in last ch, continuing working across the bottom of the foundation ch, sc in next 20 chs, 2 sc in last ch; do not join now and throughout = 46 sts

Rnd 2: 2 sc in first st of previous rnd, sc in next 20 sts, 2 sc in next 3 sts, sc in next 20 sts, 2 sc in next 2 sts = 52 sts

Rnd 3: 2 sc in next 2 sts, sc in next 20 sts, 2 sc in next 6 sts, sc in next 20 sts, 2 sc in next 4 sts = 64 sts

Rnd 4: Sc in each st around = 64 sts

Rnd 5: [Sc in next st, 2 sc in next st] 2 times, sc in next 20 sts, [sc in next st, 2 sc in next st] 6 times, sc in next 20 sts, [sc in next st, 2 sc in next st] 4 times = 76 sts

Rnd 6: Sc in each st around = 76 sts

Rnd 7: [Sc in next 2 sts, 2 sc in next st] 2 times, sc in next 20 sts, [sc in next 2 sts, 2 sc in next st] 6 times, sc in next 20 sts, [sc in next 2 sts, 2 sc in next st] 4 times = 88 sts

Rnd 8: Sc in each st around = 88 sts

Rnd 9: [Sc in next 3 sts, 2 sc in next st] 2 times, sc in next 20 sts, [sc in next 3 sts, 2 sc in next st] 6 times, sc in next 20 sts, [sc in next 3 sts, 2 sc in next st] 4 times = 100 sts

Rnd 10: Sc in each st around = 100 sts

Rnd 11: [Sc in next 4 sts, 2 sc in next st] 2 times, sc in next 20 sts, [sc in next 4 sts, 2 sc in next st] 6 times, sc in next 20 sts, [sc in next 4 sts, 2 sc in next st] 4 times = 112 sts

Rnd 12: Sc in each st around = 112 sts

Rnd 13: [Sc in next 5 sts, 2 sc in next st] 2 times, sc in next 20 sts, [sc in next 5 sts, 2 sc in next st] 6 times, sc in next 20 sts, [sc in next 5 sts, 2 sc in next st] 4 times = 124 sts

Rnd 14: Sc in each st around = 124 sts

Rnd 15: [Sc in next 6 sts, 2 sc in next st] 2 times, sc in next 20 sts, [sc in next 6 sts, 2 sc in next st] 6 times, sc in next 20 sts, [sc in next 6 sts, 2 sc in next st] 4 times = 136 sts

Rnd 16: Sc in each st around = 136 sts

Rnd 17: [Sc in next 7 sts, 2 sc in next st] 2 times, sc in next 20 sts, [sc in next 7 sts, 2 sc in next st] 6 times, sc in next 20 sts, [sc in next 7 sts, 2 sc in next st] 4 times = 148 sts

Rnd 18: Sc in each st around = 148 sts

Rnd 19: [Sc in next 8 sts, 2 sc in next st] 2 times, sc in next 20 sts, [sc in next 8 sts, 2 sc in next st] 6 times, sc in next 20 sts, [sc in next 8 sts, 2 sc in next st] 4 times = 160 sts

Rnd 20: Sc in each st around = 160 sts

Rnd 21: [Sc in next 9 sts, 2 sc in next st] 2 times, sc in next 20 sts, [sc in next 9 sts, 2 sc in next st] 6 times, sc in next 20 sts, [sc in next 9 sts, 2 sc in next st] 4 times = 172 sts

Rnd 22: Sc in each st around = 172 sts

Rnd 23: [Sc in next 10 sts, 2 sc in next st] 2 times, sc in next 20 sts, [sc in next 10 sts, 2 sc in next st] 6 times, sc in next 20 sts, [sc in next 10 sts, 2 sc in next st] 4 times = 184 sts

Rnd 24: Sc in each st around = 184 sts

Rnd 25: [Sc in next 11 sts, 2 sc in next st] 2 times, sc in next 20 sts, [sc in next 11 sts, 2 sc in next st] 6 times, sc in next 20 sts, [sc in next 11 sts, 2 sc in next st] 4 times = 196 sts

Sl st in next st. Fasten off if indicated in the pattern and check tips for assembling pillow (see Assembling Pillow).

ASSEMBLING PILLOW

Place the front and the back pieces together with WS facing each other. Work the edging as indicated for the specific pattern, inserting the hook through both pieces of fabric at the same time to join them as you go (3). Leave an opening at the end for stuffing.

Stuff the pillow firmly but do not over-stuff to prevent stuffing from showing through the fabric stitches (4). Complete the remaining stitches of the edging. Fasten off and weave in the ends.

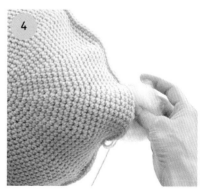

OVAL PILLOW BASE CHART

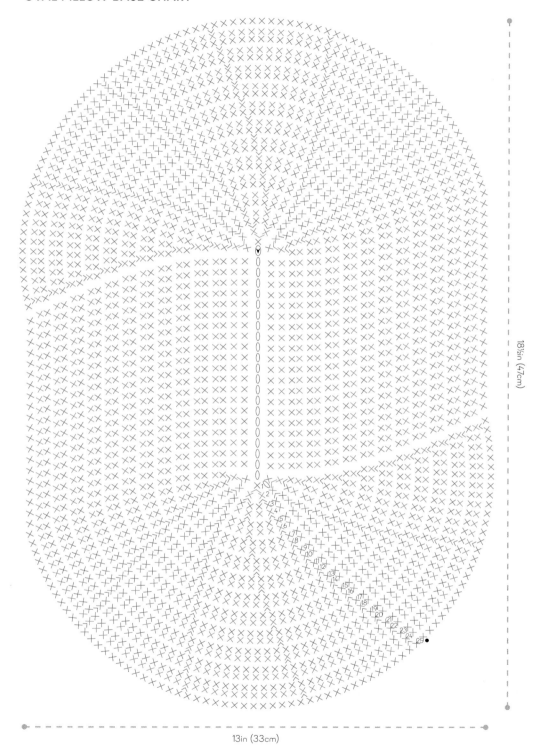

18½in (47cm)

13in (33cm)

CROCHET TECHNIQUES

COLOR CHANGE

To change yarn colors, leave the last stitch unfinished with 2 loops on the hook of the currently used color. Drop working yarn, pick up the new color and pull it through the remaining 2 loops of the previously used color (1). The last st is completed with the new color on the hook (2).

To begin the next row (or round) after a color change, crochet the first st over the previous yarn color, holding it on WS of the project (3). Continue to work as usual, following the pattern (4). This method will ensure a neat finishing of the edges and secure color changes on WS of the work.

WEAVING IN YARN ENDS

Neat finishing is the key for professional-looking work. My favorite tools for weaving in the yarn ends are (5):

- **A** – Latch hook (mid or standard gauge)
- **B** – Darning needle with latch hook eye
- **C** – Tapestry needle

LATCH HOOK

The latch hook is my most favorite tool of all. Mid or standard gauge latch hooks can be found in transfer tools for knitting machines.

Start by inserting the latch hook into the work on WS approximately 1½in (3.8cm) away from the yarn tail. Push the hook through the stitches of the row towards the yarn tail, grab the end of the tail and pull it back through the stitches (6). Now insert and push the hook through the same stitches but in the opposite direction. Grab the yarn end, skipping the last stitch and pull it back through the stitches. Repeat weaving one more time for extra security if desired. Trim the remaining tail.

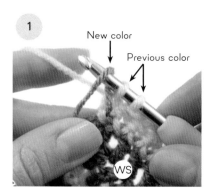

5

A B C

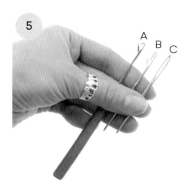

1 New color

Previous color

WS

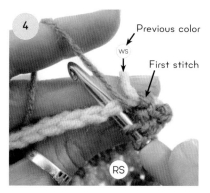

3 Previous color   New color

First stitch

RS

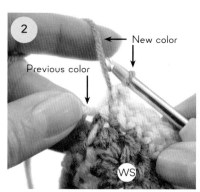

2 New color

Previous color

WS

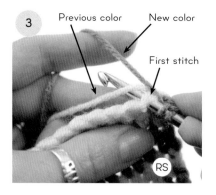

4 Previous color

WS

First stitch

RS

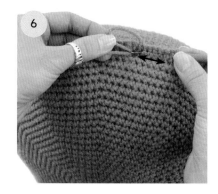

6

DARNING NEEDLE WITH LATCH HOOK EYE OR A TAPESTRY NEEDLE

A darning needle with a latch hook eye is perfect for multi-ply and bulky yarn projects. It makes threading extremely easy (7).

A basic tapestry needle is also great for weaving in any single strand of yarn.

Start by threading the yarn tail through the needle. With WS facing, insert the threaded needle into the work as close to the last stitch as possible and pull it through the stitches of the row, approximately 1½in (3.8cm) away from that point (8). Turn and run the needle through the same stitches in the opposite direction, skipping the first stitch after turning. Turn and repeat weaving one more time for extra security if desired. Trim the remaining tail.

RAW EDGE FINISHING

There are no rules on how many stitches to work in each edge stitch. Work evenly across the side stitches without over-tightening or buckling the edge. To avoid holes when working across the raw edge, insert the hook through the stitches instead of working under the stitches (9).

BOTTOM OF FOUNDATION CHAIN

By working into both sides of the foundation chain we create the beginning round (or row) of ovals and other shapes that are done in the round, as well as half ovals and other shapes that are done in rows. Complete all of the required stitches across the chain, rotate the work in a clockwise direction (or in a counterclockwise direction for left-handed crochet) and crochet along the bottom loops of the foundation chain (10 and 11).

WORKING WITH 2-3 STRANDS

If the pattern calls for working with 2 or 3 strands of yarn held together, it can be done by pulling 1 strand of yarn from individual skeins to create a group of 2 or 3 yarn strands. However, sometimes the number of available skeins is not a multiple of the required number of strands, so here are some alternative options.

DIVIDING SKEINS

Wind 2 or 3 balls out of 1 skein of yarn. Use an electronic scale to check the weight of the balls for accuracy (12).

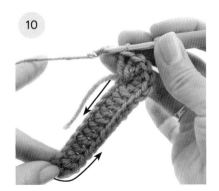
Not under the stitch
Through the stitch

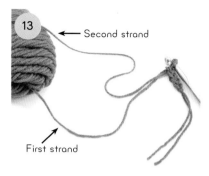

13

Second strand

First strand

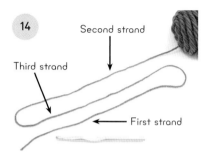

14

Second strand

Third strand

First strand

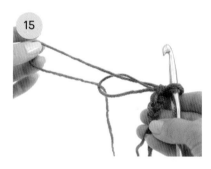

15

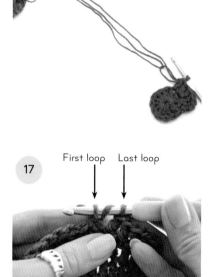

16

17

First loop   Last loop

2 STRANDS FROM 1 SKEIN

Pull the tail from the center of the skein and use the tail from the outside of the skein as the second strand. Hold these 2 ends together to crochet with 2 strands at once from a single skein of yarn (13).

3 STRANDS FROM 1 SKEIN

Fold the long yarn tail twice to triple it (14). Gather the ends and make a slipknot. Holding the 3 strands of yarn over your index finger, crochet to the end of the long loop. *Pull working yarn through the loop to create a new long loop (15 and 16). The longer the loop the better! Crochet to the end of the long loop and work the same from now on, repeating from*. This method was named "Long chain" for resembling the basic foundation chain commonly used in crochet projects.

FLAT CIRCLES

The formula for making flat crochet circles is very simple. Any double crochet circle begins with 12 stitches and increases by 12 in every round. Any single crochet circle begins with 6 stitches and increases by 6 in every round or increases by 12 in every other round. Always check the gauge and the total stitch count to ensure the correct result. Wet blocking can save the day if the finished circle does not lay perfectly flat (see General Techniques: Blocking).

If this isn't enough, it is possible to fix the gauge. If the circle ruffles, it means the stitches are too short or too wide. If the circle has a dome shape, it means the stitches are too tall or too narrow.

The height of the stitches can be adjusted by the length of the first loop that is pulled through the stitch to create a new stitch. The width of the stitches can be adjusted by the hook size or by the looseness/tightness of the last loop on the hook (17).

If your gauge is off, try to use a smaller or larger hook to obtain the gauge.

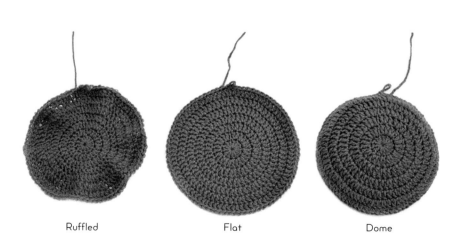

Ruffled   Flat   Dome

LEFT-HANDED CROCHET

Left-handed crocheters need not be discouraged by these patterns. Simply follow the same instructions, but work in the opposite direction. Work clockwise when crocheting in the round or from left to right when crocheting in rows. Here are a few minor notes for individual projects.

REVERSE SINGLE CROCHET

Work in the same manner as for right-handed crochet but insert the hook in the stitch to the left rather than in the stitch to the right.

GIRAFFE RUG & PILLOW

Head edge – Work sc from the left to the right corner and work rsc from the right to the left corner.

ELEPHANT RUG

Head – The trunk will be curved to the left instead of right (18).

Big circles for both ears – In Rnd 9 place **Marker A** in 14th st to the left (instead of right) and place **Marker B** in 14th st to the right (instead of left).

Small circles for both ears – After Row 6 place **Marker C** in 7th st to the left (instead of right). In Row 7 place **Marker D** in 7th st to the right (instead of left).

Assembling circles – Follow the right ear instructions for assembling the left ear circles and the left ear instructions for assembling the right ear circles. Remember, the left-handed ears and markers will be mirror images of the right-handed ears and markers (19).

Edging – Follow the right ear instructions for finishing the edge of the left ear and the left ear instructions for the edge of the right ear.

KITTY RUG

Tail – Place the tail under the left edge of the heart instead of the right edge as it will be curved in the opposite direction (20).

MONKEY RUG

Banana – Place the banana with the stem facing to the right instead of to the left as it will be curved in the opposite direction (21).

CRAB RUG

Pincers – Follow the right pincer instructions for making the left pincer and the left pincer instructions for making the right pincer.

CRAB PILLOW

Assembling pincers – Join the front and back pieces of both pincers by working sc around the edge from left to right (22).

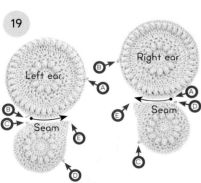

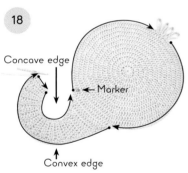

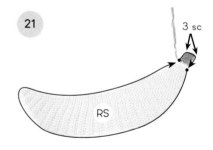

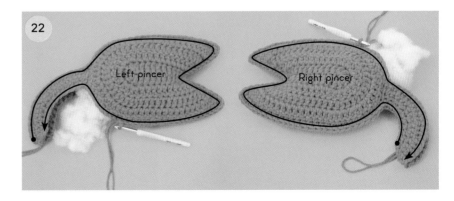

SEWING STITCHES

BACKSTITCH

CHAIN STITCH

FRENCH KNOT

1   2

STRAIGHT STITCH

WHIPSTITCH

SEWING TIPS

Always use 1 strand of yarn and a tapestry needle for sewing (unless otherwise stated).

Take extra care to pull the needle along the top layer of the fabric (not all the way through) to prevent contrasting color yarn from showing on the back of the work (1).

GENERAL TECHNIQUES

BLOCKING

Blocking is an essential finishing technique that improves the look of the stitches as well as the overall appearance of finished items. Not every project needs to be blocked, however blocking is recommended for crochet lace or advanced shapes. If the gauge is slightly off, blocking will help to remove creases and adjust the shape of crochet pieces. Spray blocking works best for heavy projects like rugs, whereas wet blocking is commonly used for light or medium weight projects.

SPRAY BLOCKING

Lay the crochet project on a blocking board. Spray the front and back of the project with warm water until it's thoroughly wet (1), stretching and shaping it to the specified measurements (2). Rotate and flip the project periodically to ensure even drying.

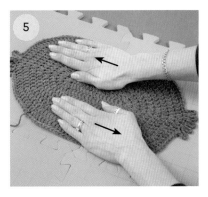

WET BLOCKING

Soak the crochet project in warm water, then gently squeeze the excess moisture out. Lay a towel onto the blocking board and roll the project in the towel to absorb extra moisture (3). Remove the towel and spread out the project on the blocking board, shaping it to the specified measurements (4). Rotate and flip the project periodically to ensure even drying.

BLOCKING TIPS

Please keep in mind that the drying process might take 2-3 hours outdoors under open sun in the summer or up to several days indoors, depending on the temperature and the humidity level.

Symmetry is very important for some patterns. The kitty face with the whiskers on each side is a good example of a symmetrical pattern. If the crochet piece turned out asymmetrical due to the personal style of crocheting, just try wet blocking and shaping (5). Try it, it really works!

NON-SLIP LINING

This lining prevents rugs from slipping. Non-slip lining is not required but is recommended for safety reasons if the rug is intended for children.

TOOLS AND MATERIALS

- Straight stitch sewing machine
- Non-adhesive shelf liner with grip or rug gripper pad
- Hook and loop tape (strip with hooks only) - 1in (2.5cm) wide
- Scissors
- All purpose sewing thread

Lay out the liner on the back of the rug and cut a rectangle that doesn't expand beyond the rug edges. Cut 4 strips with hooks from the hook and loop tape, using the measurement from the shortest edge of the liner. Place the strips evenly spaced onto the liner (6). Sew each strip around the perimeter using a straight stitch on the sewing machine (7). Roll the finished liner with the hook strips facing out. Place the lining roll at the top edge of the rug and unroll it towards the bottom edge (8). Hand press the lining to help the hooks stick to the fabric.

Gently remove the liner before washing (9). Wash the rug and the liner individually, following the care instructions on the labels of the materials used.

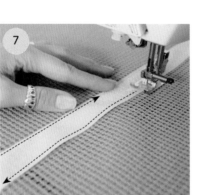

WALL DECORATION

If a crochet rug seems too beautiful to step on, why not make it into wall art? Just use the same pattern with thinner thread and a smaller size hook.

TOOLS AND MATERIALS

- Size 10 crochet thread – approximately 875yd (800m)
- 1.9mm (US size 5) steel hook
- Wall frame or poster frame, at least 3in (7.6cm) larger than the finished wall hanging on each side
- Matboard backing that fits in frame
- Matboard edging that fits in frame
- Chenille needle with sharp point
- Finger guard (thimble)
- Fabric stiffener or corn starch
- Blocking board
- Rust-proof straight pins
- Scotch tape or packing tape

Follow the pattern instructions, working with 1 strand of size 10 crochet thread and a 1.9mm (US size 5) steel hook to make a 14in x 10½in (35.5cm x 26.7cm) elephant wall hanging.

Soak the finished wall hanging in the fabric stiffener or in the corn starch mixture for 2-5 minutes (see Corn Starch Recipe).

Remove the wall hanging from the stiffener and squeeze the excess moisture out. Stretch and pin the wall hanging onto the blocking board (10), allow it to dry. It may take up to 24 hours to dry at room temperature or just a few hours in the sun.

Position the wall hanging in the middle of the matboard backing inside of the matboard edging (11).

Make a few tubes out of packing tape with the sticky side facing out (12). Use these tubes to secure the wall hanging onto the matboard backing temporarily (13).

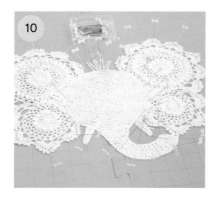

Thread the chenille needle with the crochet thread used for making the wall hanging. Attach the wall hanging to the matboard backing by basting (tacking) it around the edge (14). Make a few tiny stitches on RS between the long thread floats on WS. Remove the packing tape tubes as you go.

Tie all the ends on the back of the matboard to secure them. Insert the matboard backing with the attached wall hanging into the frame along with the matboard edging and seal the frame. Mount the frame onto the wall (15).

CORN STARCH RECIPE

Dissolve 2-3 tablespoons of corn starch in ½ cup (100ml-125ml) of cold water. Boil 3 cups (700ml) of water in a pot and slowly add the starch mixture to the boiling water, stirring it constantly for 40-60 seconds until the mixture looks clear. Remove the mixture from the heat at the boiling point and let it cool down to a temperature comfortable for hands.

ABOUT THE AUTHOR

Coming from a family of textile engineers, I was surrounded by fabrics and yarn from the time I was born. Thus working with yarn has always felt natural to me.

I learned to knit and crochet at a very young age by watching my mom, grandma and great-grandma. Crocheting along with my grandma was the happiest time of my childhood. My dad has taught me the basics of machine knitting, he could patiently answer all of my childish questions.

Over the years I learned new techniques and I developed some of my own. My earlier designs include lace dresses, skirts, tops and cardigans. Many of them were inspired by spectacular Irish crochet.

After the big transatlantic move to Canada in 2008, my design aesthetic has been transformed into a new style that I can describe as "fun creations inspired by animals".

Find Ira on Facebook: IraRott Designs

www.irarott.com

THANKS

I would like to say thank you to my wonderful husband Maurice for his endless support, to our children (Amanda, Andrew, Amy, Polina) for being so inspiring and to my parents (Serge and Elena) who are the reason why I crochet.

Also, huge thank you to all our creative team members for testing IraRott patterns. Special thanks for the additional help with this book to Carmen Carpenter, Cheryl McNichols, Courtney Knorr, Kimberly Rose, Penny Shilling, Polina MacGarvey, Ryan Nicole Hazeltine, Susan Baker and Tammy Rollston. I could not have done it without you!

SUPPLIERS

Bernat Super Value Yarn

www.yarnspirations.com

Red Heart Super Saver Yarn

www.redheart.com

General Yarn

Canada: www.michaels.com

USA: www.joann.com

UK: www.sewandso.co.uk

Worldwide: www.loveknitting.com

Stuffing and Shelf Liner

Canada: www.walmart.ca

USA: www.walmart.com

Australia and New Zealand:
www.spotlightstores.com

Worldwide: www.amazon.com

INDEX

A SEWANDSO BOOK
© F&W Media International, Ltd 2018

SewandSo is an imprint of F&W Media International, Ltd
Pynes Hill Court, Pynes Hill, Exeter, EX2 5AZ, UK

F&W Media International, Ltd is a subsidiary of F+W Media, Inc
10151 Carver Road, Suite #200, Blue Ash, OH 45242, USA

Text and Designs © IraRott, Inc 2018
Layout and Photography © F&W Media International, Ltd 2018

First published in the UK and USA in 2018

Iryna MacGarvey (Ira Rott) has asserted her right to be identified as author of this work in accordance
with the Copyright, Designs and Patents Act, 1988.

A catalogue record for this book is available from the British Library.

ISBN-13: 978-1-4463-0700-7 paperback
SRN: R7472 paperback

ISBN-13: 978-1-4463-7657-7 PDF
SRN: R7619 PDF

ISBN-13: 978-1-4463-7658-4 EPUB
SRN: R7618 EPUB

Printed in China by RR Donnelley for:
F&W Media International, Ltd
Pynes Hill Court, Pynes Hill, Exeter, EX2 5AZ, UK

10 9 8 7 6 5 4 3 2 1

Content Director: Ame Verso
Managing Editor: Jeni Hennah
Project Editor: Lynne Rowe
Proofreader: Cheryl Brown
Design Manager: Lorraine Inglis
Designers: Sarah Rowntree and Sam Staddon
Art Direction: Prudence Rogers
Photographers: Jason Jenkins and Ira Rott
Production Manager: Beverley Richardson

F&W Media publishes high quality books on a wide range of subjects.
For more great book ideas visit: www.sewandso.co.uk

Layout of the digital edition of this book may vary depending on reader hardware and display settings.